DATE DUE   JAN 0 6

MAR 09 '06			
8-22-06			
2-13-07			
GAYLORD			PRINTED IN U.S.A.

Where There's a
a
WILL

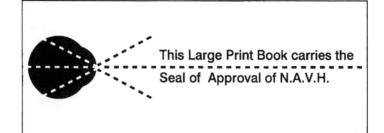

Where There's a WILL

John Mortimer

Thorndike Press • Waterville, Maine

Grateful acknowledgment is made for permission to reprint excerpts from the following copyrighted work: "A Slice of Wedding Cake" from *Complete Poems* by Robert Graves, edited by Beryl Graves and Dunstan Ward. By permission of Carcanet Press Limited.

Published in 2005 by arrangement with Viking Penguin, a member of Penguin Group (USA) Inc.

Thorndike Press® Large Print Biography.

The tree indicium is a trademark of Thorndike Press.

The text of this Large Print edition is unabridged.
Other aspects of the book may vary from the original edition.

Set in 16 pt. Plantin by Minnie B. Raven.

Printed in the United States on permanent paper.

Library of Congress Cataloging-in-Publication Data

Mortimer, John Clifford, 1923–
    Where there's a will / by John Mortimer.
      p. cm. — (Thorndike Press large print biography)
    ISBN 0-7862-8104-9 (lg. print : hc : alk. paper)
    1. Large type books. I. Title. II. Thorndike Press large print biography series.
    PR6025.O7552W48 2005b
    823´.914—dc22   2005021224

For Gus, Joe, Felix, Dora and Beatrix

Let's choose executors, and talk of wills.
— William Shakespeare,
Richard II

As the Founder/CEO of NAVH, the only national health agency solely devoted to those who, although not totally blind, have an eye disease which could lead to serious visual impairment, I am pleased to recognize Thorndike Press* as one of the leading publishers in the large print field.

Founded in 1954 in San Francisco to prepare large print textbooks for partially seeing children, NAVH became the pioneer and standard setting agency in the preparation of large type.

Today, those publishers who meet our standards carry the prestigious "Seal of Approval" indicating high quality large print. We are delighted that Thorndike Press is one of the publishers whose titles meet these standards. We are also pleased to recognize the significant contribution Thorndike Press is making in this important and growing field.

Lorraine H. Marchi, L.H.D.
Founder/CEO
NAVH

* Thorndike Press encompasses the following imprints: Thorndike, Wheeler, Walker and Large Print Press.

Contents

I

Where There's a Will

'All advice is perfectly useless,' my father told me when he sent me away to school. 'Particularly advice on the subject of life. You may, at a pinch, take your schoolteacher's word on the subject of equilateral triangles, or the Latin word for "parsley"; but remember that life's a closed book to schoolteachers, if you want my honest opinion.'

And yet the temptation to give advice is almost irresistible. From the book of Leviticus, which forbade homosexuality and the eating of prawns, through Lord Chesterfield's letters informing his son how to act like a gentleman, through Victorian doctors who advised the young that masturbation leads to blindness ('Can I just do it until I'm short-sighted?' some bright child is alleged to have asked), to present-day classes on citizenship, endless varying diets, or calls to save the universe by the segregation of rubbish, we have always been bombarded with advice. The state of the world doesn't offer much evidence of each generation having benefited from the wise words of their elders. All that could be said of a book that told the author's grandchildren how to live their lives is that it would be singularly ineffective.

'If you'll take my advice,' said the late Sir Patrick Hastings, cross-examining an habitual offender in his threatening Irish brogue, 'you'll answer the question truthfully.'

'The last time I took your advice, Sir Patrick,' the witness said, 'I got four years.'

I can think of only one piece of advice which has effectively influenced my life. When I was about seven years old I locked myself into the lavatory at the Negresco Hotel in Nice. A carpenter was called to release me. When I was extricated the hotel manager, in perfect English, said he had a word of warning for me which I should take extremely seriously. 'Let this be a lesson to you, my boy,' he said. 'Never lock a lavatory door for the rest of your life!' I never have, but this course of conduct has led to no strange encounters or indeed affected my conduct in any other way.

However, at the end of a life, there may be a natural desire to take stock of your possessions and decide what, if anything, can be dusted off and usefully passed on. Such bequests can be easily rejected as, perhaps, too familiar articles of furniture.

'Let's choose executors, and talk of wills.' So said Richard II at the time of his defeat and approaching death. And my father chose Shakespeare's line as the epigraph of his single book, *Mortimer on Probate*, still a standard work on the law governing testamentary dispositions. The cases he did in court included arguments about last wills written on a blown duck egg, or on the tail of a kite, but not, as Rider Haggard once wrote, on the naked back of a woman who had to be filed at Somerset House.

Death, in the probate cases we used to do, was the preliminary to endless family feuds, bitter recriminations and lengthy contested claims to the bedroom furniture, the elderly Bentley or the set of golf clubs. It has to be said that the deceased often encouraged this infighting by making contradictory promises to friends and relatives in order to ensure their visits and a kindly interest in a lonely old age. All the same, after twenty years spent knocking around

11

the criminal courts, it's hard to remember cases which showed human nature as more selfish, more predatory, redder in tooth and claw, than those probate actions which concerned the remnants of a finished life and the property of the dead.

What can we leave behind that will be of any use to our relatives, apart from the second-best bed, the deflated pension fund, the bundle of letters carelessly left undestroyed, the cupboard full of old suits or vintage evening dresses, the sporting prints and the doubtful Chippendale?

Having decided to make his will, W.B. Yeats announced from his tower that he had 'prepared my peace / With learned Italian things / And the proud stones of Greece, / Poet's imaginings / And memories of love, / Memories of the words of women, / All those things whereof / Man makes a superhuman / Mirror-resembling dream'. These were, no doubt, wise choices. No one is likely to start an embittered and fiercely fought legal action over the possession of a poet's imaginings, memories of the words of women or even all the things whereof man makes a superhuman, mirror-resembling dream.

And yet such bequests may be of far greater value than the seaside bungalow, the tarnished silver or the four-seater sofa. Apart from his intimate knowledge of the law of probate, my father left me his memories of Shakespeare, Browning and the Sherlock Holmes stories, together with his laughter, which I can hear quite often echoing in my children's mouths, and his sudden rages at trivial inconveniences such as cold plates, waiting for things and soft eggs. He left me, I also have to admit, his house and garden; but it's for an approach to life, a view of our brief existence suspended between two vast eternities, that I am just as grateful.

Wills are not usually places to find comments on life as it has been lived. If they are subject to prolonged and expensive interpretation, it's only to discover what items of property fall into residue or the precise effect of an act of revocation. Nor are the old, near to death, necessarily wise. Many of the greatest crimes, much of the most bigoted behaviour leading to widespread suffering and mass slaughter, have been committed by angry old people stuck, like trucks in the soft sands of the desert, in the errors of their ways. King Lear, until moments of madness brought him some illumination, had far less understanding of the human condition than the clearsighted young Cordelia. Indeed, old age can lead to panic and irresponsibility. Old men may contract near-fatal marriages or old women may fall victims to drink and cosmetic surgery. The account of accumulated wisdom may, at the end, be seriously overdrawn and an intelligent teenager may be a far more reliable guide to life than an old person with a plastic hip or a face-lift.

So where should we look, outside ourselves, for an awareness of the human condition, a country which can never be entirely explored but glimpsed, more or less widely, and penetrated in varying degrees of depth?

What can be said is that the passage of time, the addition of this or that invention, even of many scientific discoveries, has not necessarily helped towards this essential understanding. It can be argued that no writer had a clearer insight than Shakespeare, and he managed to achieve this in a world without refrigeration, Darwin, Freud, Bill Gates, e-mails, television or the mobile phone. The characters in the plays of Euripides are no less capable of revealing universal truths than those created by Eugene O'Neill or Harold Pinter. All great literature, so far as our understanding of the essential facts about ourselves goes, is modern literature.

And what is true of literature may be true of history also. The contemporary holy wars of Islam are as wrong-headed but, so far at least, less deep in blood than the Crusades. Ireland is endlessly re-enacting the days of Oliver Cromwell and William of Orange. Yugoslavs were murdering each other as a result of divisions in the Roman Empire. And yet we are busily closing our eyes to all these valuable clues. Shakespeare is dying out in schools, no one learns poetry by heart and literature seems to have begun with *Animal Farm*, *Lord of the Flies* and, perhaps, *The Hobbit*. History begins, in our schools, with the Russian Revolution or, at its most remote, the origins of the 1914 war.

So the Delphic instructions to know ourselves, Shakespeare's advice, put into the mouth of Polonius in one of the rare moments when he was being sensible, 'to thine own self be true', and Montaigne's announcement that living 'is my trade and my art' are made harder by severing relations with the past. Perhaps Yeats's bequests are, in fact, the most valuable assets we can leave, the 'learned Italian things . . . the proud stones of Greece' and, above all, 'Poet's imaginings'. These may give us wider, clearer views, but the whole truth is still unknowable. The definitive map of our universe doesn't exist. Those who think they know it all usually know the least; those who think they have all the answers have always lost the plot.

2

Changing Your Life —
and 'The Man in Sneakers'

I live surrounded by ageing rockers. Joe Brown of The Bruvvers is in the next village, Jim Capaldi of Traffic is in a nearby town, George Harrison, until his untimely death, lived in Henley, and our great friends are a beautiful pair of twins, known to us as the Heavenlies, who are married to members of the group Deep Purple. Jon Lord, the keyboard player and one of the founders of the group, has changed his life and now successfully composes classical music. One of my own changes of life is more rapid and fundamental.

I am at my first rock concert, admittedly late in life. Deep Purple, having toured the world and played to many thousands of enthusiasts in Bengal, where they were greeted with headlines like 'The Rock Heroes are in Town', are giving a concert in Oxford. The theatre is packed with an almost all-male audience, many of them playing air guitar or standing with their arms raised, swaying to the music.

I am standing in the wings, drinking champagne out of a paper cup as the band crashes triumphantly through the sound barrier. Ian Paice completes a miraculous drum solo and throws his sticks into the applauding audience with the elegance of Marie Antoinette chucking out a few cakes to the hungry mob below her windows. As I clap enthusiastically, a man standing beside me asks, 'Are you Ian Paice's dad?'

'Yes,' I say modestly. 'I'm Ian's dad and we're terrifically proud of the boy.' It was a moment of relief, a sudden escape from too many other problems. I could give up being myself and concentrate on being the delighted father of a brilliant drummer, if only for half an hour. Occasionally, meeting other rock bands and talking to drummers, I become Ian's dad again. All this only points to something else I should mention in a will, the importance, in a long life, of changing it whenever possible.

If you feel stuck in any kind of a rut you might contemplate the chameleon life of Lorenzo Da Ponte, the Jew who became a Catholic priest, the librettist of the three greatest operas ever written, the friend of Casanova, Mozzart (as he always spelled the composer's name) and two successive Austrian emperors, who married an English wife and ended up living in New York, owning an opera house and teaching Americans about Italian poetry.

In that great period of history which included the Age of Reason and the French Revolution, the world of Rousseau and Napoleon, Byron, Wellington, Shelley and Goethe, Mozart and Beethoven, Da Ponte appears in flashes of light, enjoying extraordinarily different lives in various disguises. Even his name wasn't his. The child of a Jewish family which had converted to Catholicism because, in the province of Venice, Jews were not allowed to marry, the future librettist was given the name of the bishop who baptized him.

We get a glimpse of Da Ponte in the priests' seminary at Cenada, where, in six months, he learned most of Dante's *Inferno* by heart, as well as the best sonnets and songs of Petrarch and 'the most beautiful works of Tasso'. He was fluent in Latin and became a brilliant teacher. Now we see him taking holy orders, followed by a succession of unpriestly love affairs. An anonymous denunciation accused him of an 'evil life'. Someone had seen a woman put her hand in his breeches. He fled from Venice to avoid his trial by the Inquisition and was sentenced, in his absence, to seven years in a prison cell without light.

After a tender love affair with the wife of an innkeeper, and having renamed himself for a short while with the eccentric pseudonym of 'Lesbonico Pegasio', he appears again in Vienna as 'poet' to the Burg theatre, and the favourite of Emperor Joseph II. So we find him writing libretti for three operas, one by Mozart, one by Salieri and one by Martini, feeling as he writes that 'I am reading the *Inferno* for Mozart, Tasso for Salieri and Petrarch for Martini.' He is working for twelve hours at a stretch, assisted by a bottle of Tokay on his right, his inkwell in front of him and a box of Seville snuff on his left, with a beautiful young girl, the housekeeper's daughter, to bring him a biscuit, a cup of coffee or merely her smiling face.

Da Ponte's lasting fame rests on his writing the words for *Don Giovanni*, *The Marriage of Figaro* and *Così fan tutte*. He was convinced, in these works, as in his life, that quick and complete changes of mood are essential. So, in *Don Giovanni*, scenes of farce (the changing of clothes between the Don and Leporello) are followed by moments of high comedy, tragedy and, finally, the refusal to repent, which has made Don Giovanni into an existentialist hero as he is dragged down to hell.

In *Così fan tutte* Da Ponte makes changes of identity more significant than changes of mood. The silly bet, which has caused the pair of male lovers to return in disguise to test the fidelity of their mistresses, becomes stranger and more bewildering when each mistress falls for the charms of the other's lover. Those who dismiss *Così* as a ridiculous story with deathless music seem unaware of this disturbing development. Does it, can it, mean that we are creatures without any personality, one lover, in the moment of temptation, being as good as another? In Da Ponte's libretto the possibility remains that, in the inevitable 'happy' ending, the girls actually marry the wrong partners, although this is not the way we can bear to see it performed nowadays. The pride we take in being consistent and individual souls would be far too deeply disturbed.

We can't resist a look at Da Ponte in a country house party just before the first night of *Don Giovanni.* The house was on the outskirts of Prague and the October

21

weather was still warm and beautiful. 'People lingered happily in the open air, with the feeling that days like this were a blessing,' one of the guests wrote. It was at this party that Mozart was lured into an upstairs room and the door was locked until he finished the yet unwritten over-ture. Da Ponte appears at this party with an aged librarian from the Castle of Dux. This was a man who may have been a model for the sensual Don, and who also had a rascally servant. 'Signor Casanova seems to be a really worthy old man,' one of the guests is reported to have said to Da Ponte, who replied, 'There you are making a terrible mistake. He's an adventurer who has spent his days playing cards, brewing elixirs and telling fortunes.'

After the party Da Ponte hurried back to Vienna. And the elderly Casanova, who wrote, 'the first business of my life has been to indulge my senses. I felt myself born for the fair sex', may have sat in the theatre to hear the Don tell Leporello, 'Women are more necessary to me than the bread I eat or the air I breathe.' The old man must have felt himself living again as the seducer on the stage.

Da Ponte had gone, having business to do, fresh love affairs to attend to and other opera libretti to write. He travelled to England and then turned up unexpectedly in Boston, after a terrible crossing of the Atlantic without a mattress or regular meals, to teach and sell Italian books. And then he was in New York, opening his new opera house. Some Americans objected to watching music drama sung in Italian. Da Ponte invited them to dinner, where delicious garlic-scented, succulent Italian dishes were set before them. Before they could start eating, all these delights were cleared away and replaced by bowls of American corn. The dinner also had changed identity.

Finally the opera house burnt down, but Da Ponte lived on until his ninetieth year, respected, grey-haired, still handsome and smiling through all life's changes. When he died, he had an elaborately theatrical funeral at the Roman Catholic Cathedral on 11th Street. His grave was, like Mozart's, unmarked, the cemetery has been built over and no trace of this extraordinary consumer of life exists except on the stage.

Changing the life that's been allocated to you, throwing in your hand and asking for a redeal, may require courage and determination. Our friend Derek has both. He was born the only child of two poor, totally underprivileged Jamaican immigrants in Battersea. He is now a rich and successful businessman and financial adviser, and perhaps the only black master of foxhounds in England.

Once again it's the story of a remarkable teacher, a woman at Derek's state school who liked this obviously bright little boy and invited him for weekends to her cottage in Norfolk, where he learned how to ride. When he left school, he got a job in the Attorney-General's office, made contacts and entered the world of big business. So, quick-witted and ready with an apt phrase, Derek was able to change the unpromising hand he had been dealt.

He was sailing over a fence in his full master of foxhounds regalia when a hunt saboteur shouted up at him, 'Two hundred years ago they would've been hunting you.'

'Oh yes, my dear,' Derek shouted back, 'and five hundred years ago, I would've been eating you!'

Derek is a Tory. His reason for this must be a constant accusation to those of us who are on the left, and should be a weight on the conscience of a new generation of politicians. 'When I was a poor boy in Battersea,' he said, 'and saw the way Labour treated its own people, I decided to become a Conservative.'

Hitchcock's movie *North by Northwest* has an early scene in a crowded hotel lounge. A bellboy is walking among the guests calling out that he's got a message for Mr George Kaplan. Cary Grant, who isn't Kaplan, raises his hand because he wants to make a telephone call to his mother. The villains, who have been looking for Kaplan in order to kill him, assume that Cary Grant has answered the bellboy's call and that he is, therefore, the man they're after. For the rest of the film Grant has to live the life of a stranger who turns out not to exist, avoid his assassins and share the non-existent stranger's troubles; so easy is it to slide from one identity to another.

The best of times, so far as I was concerned, was when I was both a writer and a defence barrister. The lawyer was able to learn many secrets, to meet a huge variety of people, to bear their misfortunes with great heroism and see the solutions to their problems quite clearly. Talking to juries and judges in court, I was always telling them things I thought they'd like to hear. What I thought, what I felt, was immaterial. I was someone else's voice doing my best to persuade tribunals of other people's innocence. But early, very early in the morning, before the judges, the jury members or those under arrest were awake, I was a writer trying to be entirely myself, saying exactly what I thought in a voice I hoped was no one else's.

This led to an enjoyably varied way of life. I used to spend breakfast time with a suspected murderer in an interview room in the cells under the Old Bailey, I would have lunch with the judges, who ate and drank with their wigs on at the City of London's expense, and in the evening I would have dinner with an actress. I could go, when court ended, to a rehearsal room. In doing so, I seemed to step from the world of make-believe and 'let's pretend' to the harsh reality of the theatre, where an attempt, at any rate, is being made to say something truthful about the human condition.

Most lives are long enough to play at least two parts; but the problems of identity raised by *Così fan tutte* remain. I'm writing this in Italy, and back in England a week ago Leo McKern died. He was an actor who magnificently portrayed a character I'd written, Rumpole, the claret-swigging, small-cigar-smoking, fearless upholder of our great legal principles, trial by your peers, the presumption of innocence and the rule that the police shouldn't invent more of the evidence than is strictly necessary. At a restaurant I go to near our home in England, the owner saw a newspaper headline, 'Rumpole Dies', and for days she spoke in hushed and, I'm relieved to say, regretful tones about my unfortunate death. Rumpole doesn't exist except in books and television plays. I, who wrote him, am still, unaccountably, alive. The actor who pretended to be him is dead. No wonder the newspaper headline was confusing.

And what about 'The Man in Sneakers'? I do wear trainers, gym shoes, whatever you call them, because of the state of my feet. Dressed otherwise respectably, I am in the bar of the Essex House in New York with my actress daughter, Emily, and her newly wed actor husband, Alessandro. We are with our respective families and are about to go to the opening of a film he is in. Emily moves a little away from our group to take a photograph of us all.

She is now close to a man sitting at a bar table who takes her hand and, looking at her lovingly, says, 'Sit down with me! I'll buy you drinks all the evening and liberate you from the man in sneakers.'

She disillusioned him, perhaps too soon, and told him that the man in the sneakers was her father. My change of life was short and I was no longer the well-known menace padding round New York in worn white trainers for the purpose of seducing young women.

3

Getting Drunk

I am in a broadcasting studio with a number of guests including a boy band. One of them, or one of their controllers, has just emerged from detox and everyone, including the chat-show host, is listening with the greatest respect to his account of kicking a habit. Then they turn to me. 'Have you got any addictions?' they ask. Their faces show how tolerant and understanding they are prepared to be.

'Not really,' I say. 'Except I do have my first glass of champagne around six o'clock in the morning.'

There is an awed, deeply sympathetic silence, and then the host says, 'Are you having counselling for that?'

'No,' I have to confess, 'I'm not having counselling.'

'Well, how long has this been going on?'

'Ever since I could afford to have a glass of champagne at six o'clock in the morning,' was what I had to admit.

It seems that, in classical times, drunkenness was considered a sort of higher ecstasy, such as the elevated states enjoyed by mystics, poets and lovers, in which the soul becomes separated from the body. The ecstatic behaviour of the disciples at Pentecost caused them to be accused, according to the commentaries of Erasmus, of being pissed out of their minds.

Montaigne is harder on drunkenness and more suspicious of ecstasy, but then he lived in a time when a great lord, famous for his success in several wars, never drank less than two gallons of wine at every 'ordinary meal'. Montaigne has a cautionary story of a lady with a chaste reputation who, while provocatively asleep at her fireside after drinking a great deal of wine at dinner, was impregnated by a young farm labourer without her having any idea of what was going on. So he welcomes the fact that, in his day, heavy drinking was declining, 'because we threw ourselves into lechery much more than our fathers did'.

No doubt Montaigne drank in a reasonable manner; but learning to drink can be a painful, although a necessary experience. The art master at Harrow bicycled with us to sketch the suburban countryside — a few patches of agricultural land which then existed around Ruislip reservoir — and, on the way home, we used to knock back an extraordinary number of gin and limes in the local pubs — a sickening experience. In my first term at Oxford my friend Henry Winter and I managed to drink several bowls of sherry and then boil blue Bols and crème de menthe in an electric kettle and drink the horrible result. I have to say I felt none of the higher ecstasies, nothing to compare with the out-of-body and soulful pleasure of mystics and lovers, and nothing to approach the joy of the disciples at Pentecost, nothing in fact but the nauseating sensation of a room spinning out of control. Coming back to reality, I found a theology student from next door kneeling beside me in silent prayer.

Since then no gin, lime, Bols, sherry or crème de menthe have passed my lips. I'd go so far, with Montaigne, as to say that being really drunk is not a pleasant experience, and being cornered by a drunken person who repeats every sentence at least six times is as bad as being drunk yourself, and that drunk scenes in plays or films are never funny. It's also true to say that, although crimes are committed to pay for drugs, very few crimes are committed under their influence, whereas drink, particularly a mad mixture of snowballs, vodka and pints of lager, leads to blood-stained quarrels between friends, assault and often murder.

On the other hand, a world without wine would be an extremely depressing place, and no equally enjoyable drink has ever been invented. My grandfather, a Methodist who signed the pledge and thereafter drank nothing but a temperance beverage of his own invention, which apparently produced in him all the outward and visible signs of mild intoxication, might as well have stayed with the wine. There is something strangely depressing about lunch with people who drink nothing but water. W.C. Fields said it should be avoided because fish fuck in it. What is needed is some sort of lesson in schools for intelligent drinking. Nowadays schoolchildren spend a great deal of time watching films about the evil consequences of drugs, dire warnings which seem to have little or no effect, or learning how to use the computer, which can be picked up quite simply at any age. Basic truths about how to know when to refuse another glass could be included in the GCSE syllabus.

The study of champagne might be reserved for A-levels. The French and the Italians are in dispute about its origins. According to the French, it was invented by a little monk, Dom Perignon. Italians trace this life-enhancing drink back to ancient Rome, when it was kept in urns buried in the earth. It was dark in colour and drunk qualified with water, except at orgies.

It's greeted as the 'King of all the wines' in *Die Fledermaus*, and a glass of it was taken at midday by Charles Ryder at Oxford to shock his puritanical cousin in *Brideshead Revisited*. It can cure aching legs and dispel colds, and a glass drunk to the overture of *The Marriage of Figaro* can banish depression. It's by no means a drink reserved for right-wing toffs. Trotsky was devoted to it, Chekhov called for a glass of it before his brief life ended and Nye Bevan invented the National Health Service aided by frequent bottles of it. I have been called a 'champagne socialist' (or even a 'Bollinger Bolshevik') because I think this cure-all should be made readily available on the NHS.

The study of drinking would take in a great deal of English literature, from Chaucer to Kingsley Amis, and should conclude with Byron's answer to hangovers, printed in the verses that precede *Don Juan*:

> *I would to heaven that I were so much*
>   *clay,*
> *As I am blood, bone, marrow, passion,*
>   *feeling —*
> *Because at least the past were pass'd*
>   *away —*
> *And for the future — (but I write this*
>   *reeling,*
> *Having got drunk exceedingly today,*
> *So that I seem to stand upon the*
>   *ceiling)*
> *I say — the future is a serious*
>   *matter —*
> *And so — for God's sake — hock and*
>   *soda water!*

4

The Grand Perhaps

It's notable that the list of bequests Yeats prepared in his tower didn't, in any clear way, leave his descendants any particular faith in God. He does say, 'That, being dead, we rise, / Dream and so create / Translunar Paradise.' But he has already made his view of 'Death and life' clear. 'Till man made up the whole, / Made lock, stock and barrel / Out of his bitter soul'. So, is the translunar paradise beyond the grave a creation merely of the dreams of a bitter soul? Such dreams would not have been particularly attractive to my father. 'The immortality of the soul?' he used to say. 'Isn't that rather a boring conception, like living for all eternity in some vast hotel with absolutely nothing to do in the evenings?'

I suppose we hand on what we have ourselves inherited. I received from early childhood the opinions of a Darwinian evolutionist father ('Huxley was to

Darwin,' he used to say, 'as St Paul was to Christ') and a mother who was, from her early days as an art student, a Shavian 'New Woman', a painter who had exhibited in the Paris Salon, with a head full of Clive Bell and Roger Fry and the paintings of Cézanne, and who never seemed troubled by the possible existence of any God. My father was more openly dismissive, at least of the Creation story. 'You couldn't possibly make a horse in seven days,' he told me in childhood. 'You couldn't even evolve one over seven centuries.' Accordingly I lived through my school life, and many Church of England services, unbaptized, unconfirmed and more or less quietly unbelieving. Being an only child, I had every opportunity of observing my mother and father closely and I have to say that the absence in their lives of the 'Grand Perhaps' didn't cause any deterioration in their behaviour. They didn't, so far as I could see, take to drink or lovers; they didn't, when invited out to dinner, pocket the spoons; nor did they defraud the Inland Revenue.

Far from abusing me, they trusted me with continual kindness. My mother forsook her art and devoted her life to helping my father in his blindness with as much devotion as any saint. My father, as a barrister, fought hard for his clients and carried on his practice, fixing witnesses with his clear blue, sightless eyes and remembering every date and every page in the bundle of correspondence when his world went dark. He also kept on gardening, pricking out seedlings and getting news of them, when they burst into flower, from my mother and me. Neither the loss of sight nor the approach of death caused him to turn to God.

George Eliot, who stopped going to church on principle, walked in the Fellows' Garden of Trinity College, Cambridge, solemnly speaking three words: 'God', 'Immortality' and 'Duty'. She then announced that the first was inconceivable, the second unbelievable but the third 'absolute and peremptory'. The early atheists thought good behaviour was more important, and of greater value, because it wasn't inspired by the hope of supernatural favours or the fear of any eternal punishment. I believe my mother and father had a similar sense of duty, perhaps more cheerfully expressed because my father was a great one for jokes. I suppose it was their example that made it possible for me to separate good behaviour from religious belief. It has seemed to me since that the worst crimes and cruelties can be committed by people who think they are carrying out God's will. It's hard to imagine that anyone who didn't believe they were obeying some sort of divine command could bring themselves to bury a young mother up to her neck in the sand and stone her to death for having committed adultery.

Yet no one can deny that the Christian belief in the supreme importance of each individual soul was a great advance on faiths which thought of slaves as soulless. The King James Bible is of extraordinary power and beauty, and subsequent cack-handed translations now used in churches have reduced a work of inspired poetry, said P.D. James, a woman with strong religious beliefs, to mere improbability. Much of the literature I've valued, the art I've most enjoyed, has been produced by un-questioning Christians. Whether I'm a believer or not, I'm a part of a Christian civilization.

The difficulty, as George Eliot and many others before and since her have found, is how to reconcile the existence of a loving and omnipotent God with, to give only one instance, the Holocaust. The argument that God has given us free will so we can choose to behave with ghastly cruelty and pay the bill for it in the hereafter can be applied to the Nazis who built the gas chambers and the guards who drove men, women and children into them. It falls down completely when you try to apply it to the children who were pushed down the steps to their deaths. They had no chance to exercise free will. They hadn't behaved badly. So what are they, then? To say they are simply the victims of an experiment the Almighty made when he allowed the Gestapo to do as it liked seems morally repulsive. And what about children stricken with leukaemia, teenagers dying of cancer, those who have lived impeccable and selfless lives strangled slowly to death by motor neurone disease? Free will doesn't enter this equation, the debate is about the inexplicable and apparently reckless use of omnipotence.

If this still puzzles you, I have to report that I have consulted some impressive authorities and received no very clear guidance. Cardinal Hume told me it was one of the great mysteries and it was not granted to us, nor should we ask, to know everything. This is probably the easiest way out of the difficulty. Archbishop Runcie said that every hill has a way down as well as a way up, which didn't seem to me a very helpful observation. The best reply I had came from the writer Malcolm Muggeridge, who cast God as a sort of supernatural Shakespeare, a great dramatist of the skies. 'As you know,' Muggeridge told me, 'a good play has to have heroes as well as villains, tragic as well as comic moments, piles of corpses at the final curtain instead of a happy ending.' So are good and evil merely the tools of an Almighty Playwright, eternally at his desk and thinking up new plots? Are we all, so far as God is concerned, like the 'poor player / That struts and frets his hour upon the stage'? It is, I suppose, possible, but it's not exactly a comforting explanation.

Macbeth, the creation of a mortal dramatist, takes advantage of the absence of his enemy Macduff in England to send men to his castle to murder his wife and children. All his 'pretty chickens and their dam, / At one fell swoop'. When Macduff gets this news he calls out, 'Did heaven look on, / And would not take their part?' It's a question that has, as yet, received no satisfactory reply.

It's almost dark. There's still a pale, yellowish light over the tops of black trees at the end of the border. The garden is full of children, all girls. They've been swimming in the pool and they're now eating burgers in buns, sausages in more buns, and warming their hands at the barbecue. They come from Blackbird Lees, an Oxford housing estate full of crack cocaine and crashed cars. Although their homes are quite near the countryside, they come on their holidays not knowing the difference between a cow and a lamb, and are surprised that either animal should produce the food on sale in Tesco. The girls are playing with a football which looks, in the shadows, as white as a skull. Wherever they kick it, it is retrieved and laid back at their feet by our dogs.

I have brought up the subject of George Eliot in my conversations with Paul, the ex-vicar. He is a bald, perpetually smiling, slightly deaf, former champagne salesman who has spent the afternoon taking the girls from Blackbird Lees to Legoland. He has little patience with the idea of unbelievers behaving well and doing their duty more thoroughly because it's their responsibility and not imposed by an omnipotent creator.

'Whoa!' Paul utters a cry, when in disagreement, like a man pulling at the reins of a runaway horse. 'That's altogether out of order! If atheists behave well it's because God gets behind them and makes them do it.'

So God is kind to atheists? You might have thought he would let them go to Hell in their own way, instead of which he causes them to act as an example to many of the faithful. This was, I suggested, out of character, and I remembered that Randolph Churchill, having read through the Old Testament, told Evelyn Waugh that he hadn't realized quite what a shit God was. 'Well,' I was saying to Paul, 'he was always smiting people. Of course you remember how angry he was with King Saul? He'd specifically instructed Saul to destroy the people of Amalek "and spare them not; but slay both man and woman, infant and suckling, ox and sheep, camel and ass". Saul, contrary to orders, spared the life of Agag the king and kept the best of the sheep, and of the oxen, "and of the fatlings, and the lambs, and all that was good, and would not utterly destroy them". As a result of this God repented of having made Saul king, news which caused the prophet Samuel to weep all night.'

'Whoa!' Paul called out more loudly, again reining in the galloping horse. It was a cry to which the girls from Blackbird Lees paid no attention at all. 'That's completely out of order. The Old Testament's full of mistakes, and then Jesus came and put it all right.'

'But the people who did all that smiting . . .'

'God gives us free will to make a complete bog-up of our lives. It was their choice what they did. Their choice entirely.'

'So you believe in free will?'

'Of course. God allows us that.'

'But if he's an all-powerful God, doesn't everything turn out as he's decided?'

Paul called out 'Whoa' again, understandably as this question has caused great difficulty among religious thinkers. Aquinas, who pondered these matters deeply, was sure that as every operation results from some power, the cause for every operation must be God. So if God didn't produce the Nazi murderers, at least he took no steps to stop them. This is unthinkable and yet the idea of a helpless God permitting evil is equally difficult. Is he merely, as F. H. Bradley wrote, 'not a "Creator" at all, but somehow a limited struggling sort of chap like ourselves, only bigger and better, and loves us and tries to help us, and we ought to stick to him'?

The pale yellow sky has faded over the trees. There is only light shining from the house and from guttering candles on the tables. The children are hunting in the darkness for shoes, T-shirts or a lost towel. The Reverend Paul smiles at them benevolently. The confusions through which Aquinas tried to find a way, wanting to separate the responsibility of man (the proximate agent) from that of God (the first agent), worry him not at all. The girls who are taking last swigs of Coke, last bites of beef in a bun, have had no choice but to be born, brought up, schooled in the Blackbird Lees estate, where a cow or a sheep might seem like a creature from outer space. I had done nothing to acquire the dark garden except to be born into it. So what about free will? There was a rhyme in my childhood:

There was a young man who said,
*   'Damn!*
It's born in me that I am
A creature who moves
In predestinate grooves,
I'm not even a bus, I'm a tram!'

Down at the Old Bailey I had, day in and

day out, seen sons and daughters of judges, or top barristers, punishing the sons and daughters of burglars, fraudsters and street-fighters for what must have seemed to them a natural, even a preordained, way of life. Were the elements so mixed in the Reverend Paul, the circumstances of his life so strong, that he had no option but to give up the champagne trade and devote his life to helping the poor escape conviction for debt and to taking children from violent council estates to Legoland? Is marriage a real choice? How many attractive and available people do we meet who fancy us? We don't choose our sexual preferences or cheerful or gloomy dispositions, our illnesses or, in most cases, our deaths.

One thing can be said about free will: those, like the Calvinists, who deny its existence are a depressing and disagreeable lot. Unless we can assume we are capable of making choices and controlling our destiny, laws can't function, politicians can't be held to account, great artists can't be praised or bad painters and indifferent poets justly criticized. Shakespeare was in two minds about the matter. 'As flies to wanton boys, / are we to the gods; They kill us for their sport,' said Lear. But Hamlet speaks of the first time when his dear soul was 'mistress of her choice'. It's not vanity but practical necessity that compels us to see ourselves as free spirits, capable of taking charge of our own destiny. Although our freedom in that regard may be far narrower than we often like to think.

The garden is empty now. The girls have gone and Paul has offered me his arm to help me back into the warmth and light of the house. If the atheist George Eliot was behaving more like a Christian than many Christians, if the gloomiest determinist still holds criminals responsible for their actions, how much do these age-old questions matter? Can there be a natural instinct for good behaviour, like a belief in natural justice, and if so does it matter if it shines from a divine light or has evolved from the human instinct of mutual aid? The point at which beliefs meet may be more significant, more useful to contemplate, than their sources.

I used to meet the ageing but still mischievous Graham Greene often over lunch at Felix au Port, the restaurant not far from his home in Antibes. He was persuaded of the truth of the Christian story by a passage in St John's Gospel which describes two men, St Peter and 'that other disciple', running to the sepulchre after

Mary had, in the dawn, seen that the stones at its opening had disappeared. Peter and 'that other disciple' ran together but 'that other disciple' outran Peter and arrived first. This was a detail, Graham Greene assured me, that couldn't possibly have been invented and had the very stamp of reliable evidence about it. So the story must be true.

I found this a convincing argument, and my atheism was subject to a moment of doubt, as was, at many times, Graham's belief in the 'Grand Perhaps', which is how Bishop Blougram described God in Browning's poem. As we agreed about so many things, Graham Greene quoted other lines from the same poem which seemed to sum up his religion and my atheism.

All we have gained then by our unbelief
Is a life of doubt diversified by faith,
For one of faith diversified by doubt:
We called the chess-board white, —
we call it black.

It's good to know that both the faithful and the faithless can still be playing from the same chessboard.

5

An Old Woman Cooking Eggs

To the proud stones of Greece and poet's imaginings other bequests must be added to make up the superhuman, mirror-resembling dream. I have a gallery of pictures in my head so that, if I went blind, I could still enjoy them. I would direct you to the National Gallery of Scotland, one of the least exhausting, most rewarding collections in the world that, in a few comfortably intimate rooms, contains more masterpieces to the square foot than you have the right to expect. Among the saints and great ladies, the naked beauties and the suffering martyrs, taking her rightful and honourable place is an old woman cooking eggs.

Velázquez went to Madrid in his twenties and very soon became a court painter, truthfully observing pale-lipped kings, overdressed infantas and the sad faces of the palace dwarfs. Before that he served five years' apprenticeship to a Sevillian painter whose daughter he married and, taking time off from his religious paintings, looked hard and clearly into the kitchen.

The everyday scene in the Edinburgh gallery is lit in the sort of way the painter learned from Caravaggio, so that the objects in the kitchen achieve an extraordinary significance. The old woman has an aquiline, Sevillian nose, sharp eyes, a firm mouth and grey hair. The white cloth on her head and shoulders falls in soft folds on the coarse material of her dress. She has the suntanned, loose-skinned hands of her age but one of them holds an egg carefully and the other delicately points a small wooden spoon, ready to drip a little oil in which we can see eggs setting, their yolks and whites clear in the pan. An unsmiling peasant boy is carefully dripping in more oil and the old woman watches him anxiously. The miracle of the painting is the exact and loving re-creation of oil, eggs and earthenware, the shine on the brass pots, the shadow of a knife on a china dish, the feeling of flesh and cloth. Forget all concerns about blessings or terrifying events occurring beyond the grave, this picture celebrates the significant moment when the eggs start cooking and another spoonful of oil has to be dribbled in.

The old woman, or someone very like her, turns up again in another of Velázquez's kitchen scenes, this time in London's National Gallery. Her head is again covered with a white cloth and she is instructing a sulky and unwilling Martha on how to pound garlic and cook some fresh fish and more eggs. In a mirror we can see that Jesus has arrived at the door and is about to engage the no-doubt-eager Mary in a conversation about life, death and the miracle of salvation. Far more interesting to the old woman is seeing that the fish is cooked properly, dinner is on the table in time and the garlic is well pounded.

Velázquez went on to paint grander scenes. Venus, the Goddess of Love, lies naked, admiring herself in a mirror held up by Cupid, presenting to us her splendid bottom. He painted kings on prancing horses and military triumphs such as the surrender of Breda and royal persons hunting wild boar. He became famous in Italy for his portrait of Pope Innocent X, a merciless military commander. His final act was to decorate the Spanish Pavilion on the Isle of Pheasants for the marriage of the Infanta Maria Theresa.

Through all these great events, wars and festivals, the lives of kings and Popes, the old woman remained busy in the kitchen, dealing with the important things in life, such as the exact amount of olive oil needed to fry eggs.

6

The Domino Theory and the
Tyranny of Majorities

Avoid those whose views on every subject can be confidently predicted after you have discovered what they think about one. You know, with some people who utter dire threats about global warming, for instance, that they are going to be hostile to smokers, motor cars, jokes about mothers-in-law, school nativity plays, strip shows and the swallowing of live oysters. Equally tedious are those who complain about high taxes and are bound to be in favour of the death penalty, take a tough line on asylum seekers and are hostile to gay weddings, homeopathic medicines, Muslims and conceptual art.

'Our interests,' Browning wrote, 'are on the dangerous edge of things / The honest thief, the tender murderer / The superstitious atheist'. Characters without contra-

52

dictions are like eggs without salt. They have failed to work out what they really think about all these great or trivial matters and meekly accept the rule that pushing over one domino will lead to the collapse of a whole line of others. Surprising beliefs are the most precious. Enoch Powell, for instance, at least had a mind that went beyond dominoes. Thought of as a racist because he made his 'rivers of blood' speech, warning of violence as a result of mass immigration, he was, surprisingly, passionately opposed to the death penalty. In his somewhat strangled voice, he said that there was no evidence that hanging had any effect on the murder rate and that it was an 'avoidable brutality' in a world in which we have quite enough unavoidable brutalities to contend with. He was also against listening to music. 'I don't like things,' he explained, 'that interfere with one's heartstrings. It doesn't do to awaken longings that can't be fulfilled.' He also resented Harold Wilson for having given up power voluntarily. He had always admired Diocletian for doing this very thing, but Harold Wilson, for Enoch Powell, had somehow spoiled or cheapened the great Emperor's gesture. Although no admirer of trade unions, he said he would willingly raise his hat to any union leader who had been promoted to the House of Lords, 'if I happened to recognize him and was wearing a hat at the time'. This eccentric collection of opinions was too much for party politicians, who like a straightforward game of dominoes, and Enoch Powell, the only politician since the war who could write Greek verse while sitting on the front bench, had a career which ended in deep disappointment.

We now have a New Labour government that not only has the whole range of politically correct opinions, but is tempted to enforce them by law against those with contrary views. Beliefs about how you live your life, matters of private decision, views best kept for private enjoyment, prejudice or entertainment, can't be imposed by the operation of the criminal law. Attempts to enforce such views can only make a government the subject of ridicule.

The sort of conduct that should be subject to the law was well defined by John Stuart Mill. Mill was an extraordinary character. His father, the son of a shoemaker, was a Scottish philosopher. Thanks to him, John Stuart learned Greek at the age of three but had to wait until his eighth year before he conquered Latin. By the time he was thirteen, he had more than a working knowledge of logic and political economy. Grown to manhood, he always started his day's work at the offices of the East India Company with tea, bread and butter, and a lightly boiled egg. He wrote incessantly on political economy, on poetry, history and religion. He was a botanist who played the piano and was greatly afflicted by melancholy. He was also deeply in love with his wife, the former Mrs Taylor, whom he regarded as a superior being. When he published his essay *On Liberty*, he wrote:

The sole end for which mankind are warranted, individually or collectively, in interfering with the liberty of action of any of their number, is self-protection. The only purpose for which power can be rightfully exercised over any member of a civilized community against his will is to prevent harm to others. His own good, either physical or moral, is not sufficient warrant. He cannot rightfully be compelled to do or to forbear because it will be better for him to do so, because it will make him happier, because in the opinions of others to do so would be wise or even right. These are good reasons for remonstrating with him, or reasoning with him, or persuading him, or entreating him, but not for compelling him, or visiting him with any evil in case he do otherwise. To justify that, the conduct from which it is desired to deter him must be calculated to produce evil to someone else.

Another sentence from Mill seems to me of the greatest importance: 'Over himself, over his own body and mind, the individual is sovereign.' So what we do to ourselves, what we smoke, eat or drink or say, is entirely our own affair. We can spend our lives risking our necks mountain climbing or skiing, wolf down chocolates and read trashy novels, pursue great love affairs or sit staring contentedly into space, work out in the gym or forswear all exercise, and it's absolutely nothing to do with the government.

When governments say that they have a majority on their side when attempting to enforce a particular view of life upon those who don't happen to agree with them, they should remember Mill on the tyranny of majorities. A democracy isn't judged by the number of times a majority gets its own way but by the freedom allowed, and the respect paid, to the rights of minorities. But society too can try to impose some deadening uniformity by the despotism of the opinion of the majority. 'It presumes to tell men what to think or read, it discourages spontaneity and originality, strong character and unconventional ideas,' Mill wrote. 'Society . . . practises a tyranny more formidable than many kinds of political oppression, since . . . it leaves fewer means of escape, penetrating much more deeply into the details of life, and enslaving the soul itself. Protection, therefore, against the tyranny of the magistrate is not enough; there needs protection also against the tyranny of the prevailing opinion and feeling.'

When he was almost sixty John Stuart Mill, apparently to his surprise, was elected to Parliament as a 'working man's candidate' for Westminster. He made himself unpopular by campaigning for women's suffrage and writing an essay on *The Subjugation of Women*. He also became a secular godfather to the Earl of Amberley's second son, whose name was Bertrand Russell. Eight years later he followed his beloved wife to their grave in Avignon. The memory of Mill, and what he wrote, should be handed on in the wills of every generation.

Leave Country Sports Alone, an organization of Labour supporters in favour of foxhunting, is a cause which has the great advantage of flouting the domino theory and defying the social and legal diktats of New Labour thinking. The many decent and reasonable people who enjoy foxhunting — and the many more who dislike the idea of it intensely — will never agree. What is important is that one side shouldn't enforce its views by the use of the criminal law. Dragging the many middle-aged women and pony-club girls who hunt off to our overcrowded prisons would be an absurdity. Hunting would seem to fall within Mill's definition of an area in which the law should not interfere with the way in which you or I wish to lead our lives. It does no harm to other persons — unless you wish to count a fox as a person, which leads you into anthropomorphic arguments or the world according to Disney.

Mainly, it seems, to placate its backbenchers, denied any power and restless at its conservative behaviour, the government is threatening to introduce a bill to ban hunting. Four hundred thousand assorted country dwellers marched through London to protest at this, and what they feel is a general neglect of farming and the countryside. Not much good at marching, I was invited to lead the wheelchair battalion.

I was given an electric wheelchair, a sort of battery-operated scooter with a seat, in which I was supposed to lead the small army of the handicapped. They were lined up on the Embankment and we were found a space to join the long column of marchers.

I suppose I shouldn't have been surprised to find that the occupants of motorized wheelchairs are intensely competitive. As soon as we got going, they speeded up and challenged me for the lead. A very large lady in a bright red and powerful wheelchair drew up alongside. She was driving a Rambler, she said, which could cross country and in which she had ascended Mount Snowdon. There was room for eight bottles of wine under the bonnet of this remarkable vehicle and during the Jubilee celebrations the police had attempted to arrest her on the suspicion that she was drunk in charge of her wheelchair. They invited her to get out of it and join them in the station, but when she told them that it would take at least eight strong officers to lift her out of the Rambler they decided, wisely, to let her go on her way.

So we sped along the Embankment, under the bridges where the crowds waved at us and the police clapped; and the mounted police, who are often seen on the hunting field, were also approving. There have been left-wing hunters, Trotsky and Engels and, in my youth, Reggie Paget, a well-known Labour MP who rode to hounds. Trollope and Siegfried Sassoon, no right-wing bigots, wrote glowingly of the sport. But the large woman in the Rambler, who could never clear a fence or draw a covert, once cheerfully tipsy in charge of her wheelchair, turning out to protest against a ban on hunting, seemed to me an excellent example of someone who refuses to be submerged in the values of the majority. Whatever you might think of her, you could never have predicted her views like a row of dominoes.

7

Outdoor Sex

'She crawled with a rustle of grass towards me, quick and superbly assured. Her hand in mine was like a small wet flame which I could neither hold nor throw away. Then Rosie, with remorseless, reedy strength, pulled me . . . down, down into her wide green smile and into the deep subaqueous grass.'

I should include in my will a strong recommendation of the joys of alfresco sex, as described by Laurie Lee when he tasted kisses and cider. Recently our New Labour government introduced a comical bill into Parliament which would ensure that in future Laurie and his Rosie would end up in the nick for making love in a public place.

'The first of May, the first of May, outdoor fucking starts today,' went an old American rhyme. Not if the New Puritans in power had their way it wouldn't, not on the first of May or any other time this spring. The lovers and their lasses were about to be cracked down on.

Mr Blunkett, the Home Secretary, is not a man unfamiliar with poetry. He must surely have read *Cider with Rosie*, Laurie Lee's sun-filled bucolic memoir. He even took part in Laurie's memorial service and spoke highly of that poet and great celebrator of love in the cornfields. He must remember, too, Shakespeare's lover and his lass

That o'er the green corn-field did pass,
In the spring time, the only pretty
*   ring time,*
When birds do sing, hey ding a ding,
*   ding;*
Sweet lovers love the spring.

Why on earth should Mr Blunkett, or Hilary Benn, son of Tony Benn, the great firebrand of the left, who is the Home Secretary's junior minister, seek to confine the sweet lovers to Wormwood Scrubs, where very few birds can be heard singing?

There can be few people who, looking back on happy moments of their lives, can't remember love in the open air. It wasn't a cornfield perhaps, but the edge of a wood, or a warm beach at night with the gentle sound of waves retreating.

My own, long-ago introduction to sex was late at night, in the bracken on the common, after we had collected glow-worms in our handkerchiefs. After all these years I find myself waiting the arrival of the police.

The countryside in summer has always been the place for love:

Someone stole my heart away,
Riding in a load of hay . . .
Heather beds are soft —
And silken sheets are bonny,
But I would give it all
To go with my man Johnny.

Hearts were broken 'coming through the rye'. Hayricks and long grass were thought of as just as romantic and far more suited to the occasion than silken sheets and soft mattresses, and were no doubt a great deal healthier than dubious lunchtime hotels, places which were not available to most country lovers and their lasses.

Now it has been suggested that not only cornfields and commons should be out of bounds. You wouldn't even have been able to make love in your own garden if the Sexual Offences Bill had become law.

Frustrated couples would have had to confine themselves to weeding in a sexy way, or mowing the lawn with smothered eroticism. Love on the lawn was to be made a criminal offence. 'Come into the garden, Maud', even if the 'black bat, night, has flown', could only be an invitation to admire the dahlias. Not only had the government decided to tell us how to behave in our own gardens, but love in cars, the subject of many happy teenage memories, was to be added to the ever-growing list of New Labour crimes.

I remember my father, a prominent and successful divorce lawyer, coming home to me in my nursery and telling me that he had had a great success in proving adultery when 'really the only evidence we had was a pair of footprints upside down on the dashboard of an Austin Seven motor car parked in Hampstead Garden Suburb'. Such adultery, no doubt calling for a good deal of athletic skill, was not only to be grounds for divorce but the subject of a criminal conviction. Sex in any place that could possibly be described as 'public' was to be banned outright.

A difficult question arose with regard to the mile-high club. There is something about air travel, a rush of adrenalin caused by a mixture of fear, business-class champagne and the excitement of foreign travel, which so turns people on that they are tempted, once they have struck up an acquaintance with a person of the opposite sex in the next seat, to suggest a joint visit to the lavatory not too long after the safety belt sign has been switched off.

This might, after long legal argument, be held to be a private act. What about the couple in a well-known London club whose eyes met across the dining room so lovingly that the man suggested they repair to the facilities downstairs? When the lady replied, 'Your place or mine?' and he went for hers, they would have been committing no crime, because the newly suggested law, according to the young Benn, would have determined that sex in lavatories might be all right if the door is kept closed. What is there left to say about a government bill which suggests that love in the loo is OK, but do it in a cornfield and you've committed a serious crime?

So the car parks and the lay-bys in which some vehicles may be gently rocking would have been subject to police raids. I remember when our car broke down, late at night, on our way home to our house in the country. Knocking politely on the window of a Volvo parked on the edge of a wood where a couple were preparing to make love, I asked them for a lift. With extraordinary kindness they drove us home. When they had done so I offered them the hospitality of a spare bedroom. They said no, they preferred their own car and the dark corner of the wood. They were, of course, hardened criminals.

The thinking behind these proposals, if they could be dignified with such a word, was that the great British public must be spared the sight of anyone making love. It's true that, while making love is extremely enjoyable, watching other people doing it is not such a great treat. But are we to assume that the public is incapable of averting its eyes or passing quickly by? Are we bound to peer into every parked car or gaze into every garden, hoping for a shock?

When we won the last war, when VE Day was declared, Hyde Park was covered with ecstatic couples having sex. It would have been a night of celebration for New Labour's police. But now you would have to take a good deal of trouble, and perhaps a detour, to see an act of love. In a long life, I can't say I remember many occasions when I have stumbled on a couple locked in an intimate embrace. If I had, I don't see why it should have caused me any particular distress.

The vast majority of films and a great deal of television today portray acts of simulated sex, so the British public must, by now, at least know what it looks like. It wouldn't come as a great shock to anyone even if they happened upon it in the cornfields or noticed it, as I believe you sometimes can, in the showers attached to the Houses of Parliament.

We live, as I'm writing this, in the most extraordinary times. Our prisons are so overcrowded that there is no room in them, apparently, for burglars. The courts are overworked, the Crown Prosecution Service is near to breakdown and yet the lover and his lass, arrested in the cornfield, might have been sent to jail.

So I leave you the memories and possibilities of woods and fields, the corners of churchyards or the back seats of Toyotas. In his wise and beautiful book, Laurie Lee writes of country life when he got to know Rosie: 'It is not crime that has increased, but its definition. The modern city, for youth, is a police-trap. Our village was clearly no pagan paradise, neither were we conscious of showing tolerance . . . The village neither approved nor disapproved, but neither did it complain to authority.'

The government's proposals to ban outdoor sex provoked such hostility and derision among the saner members of the House of Lords, where the bill was introduced, that they will have to be dropped. Other strange provisions of the Sexual Offences Bill, however, remain. It will, from now on, be a serious crime to have sex with anyone with learning difficulties. You should therefore prepare a short examination paper for your partner as part of the foreplay. If he or she fails to pass, the gig will have to be off. Even if your girlfriend can find her way easily through Proust in French, you will have to satisfy the court that she hadn't a speech defect which might prevent her from saying, 'No.' It will also be a sad day for those with learning difficulties, who won't be allowed to have sex with anyone else, including other people with learning difficulties.

Finally, the bill contains a new offence of oral rape. This led one peeress, during the debate, to ask plaintively, 'Have women no longer teeth?'

Enough of sexual offences. Let's all go out into the garden.

8

Shakespeare's Favourites

Shakespeare, like Richard II, talked of wills and famously left his second-best bed to his wife. He left no advice, however, rightly believing that it's a dramatist's business to ask questions and not provide answers. His characters speak their own thoughts and not his, but perhaps we get closest to him when we hear the voices of those that he loved the most. They were not the kings and queens or even the princes, the great heroes and heroines, the giants with a fatal flaw or the star-crossed lovers, who had, he said, a great deal in common with poets and lunatics. No, the characters he loved were the men and women of common sense, clear heads, loyal, stoical, able to see through the mists of self-delusion and deceit out of which great tragedies come.

They don't have starring roles, but they are the best friends of the heroes or heroines and if only they were listened to much trouble might be avoided. One such character, clearly loved by the author, is Kent, true to King Lear as he lives through his master's reign from arrogance to madness and gentle resignation. 'I do profess to be no less than I seem;' says Kent in his creed. To 'serve him truly that will put me in trust; to love him that is honest; to converse with him that is wise, and says little; to fear judgement; to fight when I cannot choose; and to eat no fish.'

Another embodiment of the loyal and truthful man of common sense is, of course, Horatio, of whom Hamlet said:

> . . . thou hast been
> As one, in suffering all, that suffers
>   nothing,
> A man that fortune's buffets and
>   rewards
> Hast ta'en with equal thanks . . .
> Give me that man
> That is not passion's slave, and I will
>   wear him
> In my heart's core, ay, in my heart
>   of heart,
> As I do thee.

After which Hamlet, thinking he has expressed himself too emotionally to be the stoical character he so much admires, says, 'Something too much of this . . .' Perhaps our problem today is that we have too many Hamlets and not enough Horatios.

Kent, Horatio, the favoured character turns up again and again in more complex forms as, for instance, Enobarbus in *Antony and Cleopatra* or the more cynical Lennox in *Macbeth*. When Owen Glendower, the Welsh wizard, says 'I can call spirits from the vasty deep' and Hotspur replies 'Why, so can I, or so can any man; / But will they come when you do call for them?' the dashing young hero becomes one with the common-sensible enemy of pomposity and pretension. Emilia, Iago's clearsighted wife, can berate the murderously jealous Othello, 'O gull! O dolt! As ignorant as dirt!' and express the common sense of the audience, cutting the heroic, poetic, easily deceived Moor of Venice down to size so that we can be allowed to feel some sympathy for him at the end of the play. There is a great deal of this straight-talking spirit in Rosalind, and Juliet's loquacious and boring old nurse has more good sense in her little finger than the Franciscan confessor Friar Laurence has, with his dotty plans calculated to cause a tragedy, in his entire body.

This stoical character, who can survey the vagaries of the world with a smile of tolerant amusement, until some mindless horror makes him or her call out, 'O dolt! As ignorant as dirt!', comes close to that adopted by Michel, Lord of Montaigne, another writer with a tower, his shelves crammed with books and his walls covered with quotations from Greek and Roman philosophers. He did his best to incorporate the stoical attributes of the great past civilizations into the Christianity of the Renaissance and to discover 'a sane and decent manner of life'. John Florio, who translated Montaigne, was undoubtedly a friend of Shakespeare and there is, in the British Museum, a copy of Florio's Montaigne with Shakespeare's name, some say in his handwriting, written in it. Whether *The Essays* influenced the later plays, or confirmed Shakespeare's feeling for his favourite characters, the views of the glovemaker's son from Stratford and the heir to the country round the vineyards of Château Eyquem echo each other, and add their valuable bequests to succeeding generations.

Montaigne wrote little about the afterlife but he was concerned to reconcile the humanist to the process of dying. 'I want death to find me,' he wrote, 'planting my cabbages — caring little for it and even less about the imperfections of my garden.'

9

Listening

The world's full of talkers, with not nearly enough listeners. This leads to many lonely people wandering from room to room in their quiet empty houses, asking and answering questions from and to themselves. Too many of us rabbit on about ourselves, repeating what we know already, and fail to discover anything about the curious lives and the unopened histories of the passenger in the corner seat, the sad-eyed, lonely drinker at the end of the bar or the apparently ill-assorted couples in the holiday hotel.

The art of listening is one that has to be learned by lawyers. You may think of Rumpole's life as one of incessant chatter, forever up on his hind legs making speeches or asking questions. Yet a good half of a barrister's life is spent listening in silence in his chambers room or during a prison visit.

It was as a divorce barrister that I learned of the hotelier husband who fixed up a lengthy trough from his bedroom window to the vegetable garden, so that he could urinate in comfort and water the runner beans at the same time. This device caused embarrassment to the hotel's visitors who were taking tea in the garden. His wife, not unnaturally, wanted to end the marriage. At the trial the husband asked if he might give evidence standing on his head. This request was curtly refused. I heard from the lady who joined a wife-swapping club in Croydon, 'mainly to give my husband some sort of interest in life' and fell deeply in love with her swap. I learned more than perhaps I needed to know about the husband who armed his children with lavatory brushes and put them through small-arms drill with these implements every morning before sending them off to school. I also heard much of the husband who would write letters to his wife's furniture which he then pinned to it, such as, 'You are a cheap and vulgar little sideboard. Please return to whatever bargain basement you came from! You are certainly not wanted in this establishment.'

I listened carefully to the elderly man who carried out a number of alleged 'mercy killings' who told me his evidence would be given by his 'puppet master', who would speak through a hole in my client's head. I defended a certain Anthony Sorely Cramm, of whom the judge said, 'Best name for a bugger I ever heard', and, being in a merciful mood, said he might go instead of prison to a Salvation Army hostel, at which Mr Cramm called out in desperation from the dock, 'For God's sake, send me to prison!' I learned how a talented artist came to invent a non-existent Victorian photographer and forged a large number of photographs of the slum children of Victorian London which completely fooled the National Portrait Gallery. I also heard the story of a rich young man who, when asked what he had done when he stabbed his mother, said, 'I have either murdered a prostitute or killed a peacock in paradise.'

But strange, almost unbelievable stories are not available only to lawyers. They are all around you if you are prepared to listen. After a brief acquaintance a friend told me that, when he was a youngish boy, his mother left his father. The father, a correct and presumably sane army officer, told his son that his mother was dead. This is what he believed until he was in his late twenties, and was staying in a house in Scotland. There was a grey-haired woman there who was married to an air vice-marshal. After dinner she took my friend aside and told him she was his mother but it would embarrass her husband if he found this out, so would he please call her 'auntie'. Another casual friend told me that when he was a small boy his father came to his bedroom and said, 'I found this chap had been making love to your mother, so I shot him. I hope that's all right.' He then switched off the light and left the room.

It's not only friends, however casual, but total strangers who, in the first chance encounter, have told me about their unhappy marriages, their request to God for advice on divorce and even about the size, often a disappointment to them, of their virile members. All that is needed to open the floodgates is a look of rapt attention and an opening request which can be as unsubtle as, 'Do please tell me the story of your life.' Ten to one, no one has ever asked them this and they've been longing to tell it.

All this will be of great assistance to you if you're thinking of going in for the business of writing; at least it will convince you that there is no such thing as an ordinary life. Such encounters may be of even more direct assistance. I found myself sitting at lunch next to a grey-bearded, energetic-looking man who started the conversation by asking me a question. 'What do you do,' he said, 'when your boat meets a force eight gale in the Channel — what do you do with your female crew?'

I confessed that I had no experience of yachting and asked him what *he* would do.

'Double my fist, punch her on the chin and stun her.' He spoke as though it was the most obvious course to take. 'If she's unconscious she's far less likely to slip overboard.'

'And what do you do when she wakes up?'

'Get her to make a cup of tea.'

It was time to ask if his sport of yachting wasn't extremely dangerous.

'It's not dangerous at all if you can't swim,' he told me. 'If you can swim you try to swim to the shore and invariably drown. If you can't swim, you cling to the wreckage and they'll send out a helicopter for you.' So he gave me the title of a book called *Clinging to the Wreckage*. It was at the same lunch table that an elderly man, who had remained silent throughout the meal, suddenly asked me, in a loud voice, if I could get my gamekeeper to eat rooks.

So there's no better occupation than listening, only interrupting to ask for further and better particulars. An acquaintance came up to me with a friend and asked if I knew 'Baghdad Price'.

'No, I don't know Mr Price,' I had to confess, and was lucky enough to ask why he was called 'Baghdad'. Did he perhaps come from Iraq?

'No. It's just that he's a most terrible shot. And when out shooting once he shot his father by mistake. So they call him Bag Dad.'

There aren't many Iraqi jokes around at the moment, so this was one worth listening for.

10

Believing in Something

We used to have them — once we had them quite seriously — passionately held political beliefs. In England, at least; perhaps in Europe and America, they disappeared long ago. You could, I suppose, say that a cure has been found and, like tuberculosis and scurvy, we no longer suffer so badly from them. Or you might take the view that they have just gone out of fashion, like waistcoats and long johns. For whatever reason, they are certainly not around much any more. It's difficult to know, in these grey days, when the left has become the right, what sort of political beliefs, if any, I could hand on to another generation which has shown, so far, an almost passionate lack of interest in the subject.

We certainly had political beliefs when I was young, and got them as inevitably as measles and chickenpox and other long-lasting infectious diseases. The world seemed so simple then. The right, in the shape of Nazis, Fascists and those Conservatives who tolerated them, was indisputably evil. The noble left was for liberty, socialism and the rights of man. An added attraction, for those of us who were growing up in public schools, was that the left was, on the whole, in favour of the abolition of these uncomfortable and, we believed, class-ridden institutions.

But my political beliefs began before I arrived at Harrow. I was at a preparatory school at the time of the war in Spain, which seemed a clear conflict of the goods versus the bads. It was also an age when a great part of the map was coloured pink, and I wrote poems expressing my contempt for the British Empire and the works of Kipling, both of which attitudes I have now lived to regret. I read Orwell and Auden and Hemingway, and I saw myself in Spain, bumping in a bullet-holed car across a dusty orange grove with a gun in one hand and a guitar in the other, prepared to die fighting the Fascists.

When I got to Harrow I did become, encouraged by a circular from Esmond Romilly, Jessica Mitford's husband, who was anxious to stir up a spirit of rebellion in public schools, a one-boy Communist cell, and I got puzzling and contradictory instructions from party headquarters in King Street when Stalin and Hitler were, for a short time, allies, until Germany invaded Russia. I first saw London burning from Harrow churchyard and, although the prospect of reaching a respected old age seemed dicey, we never doubted, even when France fell, that Fascism would eventually be defeated.

I spent the war in a government film unit writing scripts and joining the union. So at meetings I got called 'Comrade' and 'Brother', which was a great improvement on school, when I was 'Mortimer' or 'Boy' when they wanted me to clean their shoes. We added to our simple belief that the Nazi hordes would be defeated the hope that, when peace returned, there would be a new classless society, with free dentistry, free milk for schoolchildren and jobs for all. In short, we longed for the return of a Labour government. Much to our amazement, our wishes were granted.

Looking back down the long corridor of the years, I can't remember England ever being so united as it was during the war, or so hopeful as during the Attlee government. It was the world dreamed of by those who took part in army education schemes and who read *Penguin New Writing* and the *New Statesman*. It introduced the welfare state and dented, although it couldn't destroy, the class system. It did sensible deals with various unions. Nye Bevan became our favourite politician, a silver-tongued, champagne-drinking reformer who loved the arts and enjoyed parties. Politics had changed, to conform to some of our dearly held beliefs.

Many of these achievements survived during subsequent Conservative governments. The welfare state continued, the Health Service appeared to work and trade union leaders were invited in for beer and sandwiches, not treated like dangerous revolutionaries who undermined the state. Then came the Sixties, and the flower power children, offered new exotic delights, not unnaturally lost interest in domestic politics and found Harold Wilson and James Callaghan unexciting figures compared with Mick Jagger, Dr Timothy Leary and the Bhagwan.

Some sort of consistency remained, however, until the advent of Mrs Thatcher, when beliefs, strong and strident, re-entered the world of politics. She believed totally in the ethics of the corner shop, the values of the marketplace, the dribbling down of prosperity from the seriously rich to the less fortunate classes and the unreliability of foreigners.

In these circumstances, of course, those of us on the leftish side of politics had our beliefs strengthened and our faith increased. No doubt there could be, there undoubtedly had to be, a better way, liberal, humane, concerned with justice, equality and the pursuit of happiness, with perhaps still a little socialism in it. All this would come about with another Labour government.

And then the politicians of the left, both in England and in America, performed a surprising somersault. They became Conservatives. This, they no doubt thought, was rather a clever thing to do. It meant they could appeal to a basically Conservative electorate and leave right-wing politicians gasping for breath, lost for words and with absolutely nothing to complain about. It also had the effect of leaving the left's longtime supporters disenfranchised, disappointed and understandably confused. No doubt the new leadership thought that such party faithfuls would vote for them anyway, so their old-fashioned principles could be safely ignored.

Now we have watched a Labour government with a huge majority behave as though the word 'liberal' were a term of abuse and 'human rights' an easy way out for criminals. It has sought to diminish trial by jury, chip away at the presumption of innocence by introducing evidence of previous convictions and has abolished the principle of double jeopardy. It proposes to imprison suspected terrorists and the mentally sick without trial. It contemplates returning refugees to countries where they may face torture, in contravention of our obligations under the Convention of Human Rights. I was recently talking to Michael Heseltine, once the Tarzan of the rightwing jungle. I asked him if he was still active in any way in politics. 'Not really,' he said. 'We've got a Conservative government in power, so why should I worry?' Politicians do make it very hard to have deeply held political beliefs.

There are certain principles, however, which have to be clung to in spite of party loyalty or the contortions of politicians. The rights of man, fair trials and justice for the poor and oppressed have to be maintained, regardless of the discouragement and disillusion which go with the fight for all liberal causes. These are attacked, as we have seen, by those who advertise their left-wing credentials. Such concerns may not be the whole of a life and may be an unexpected part of it. In this context, it might be interesting to consider the often-ignored political conscience and concerns of Lord Byron.

I first got to know Byron because we went to the same school, not at the same moment of history, but his dagger and his Turkish slippers were still in the library and I tried to lie on that grave in Harrow churchyard where he lay to write poetry. An iron grille made the stone hard to lie on, and the suburban view is not as inspiring as it no doubt was in his day.

In the business of leaving, to my heirs and assigns, poet's imaginings, I couldn't leave out the poet whose great acts of imagination undoubtedly included himself. The wonder and lovable quality of Byron is that, having cast himself as a beautiful but damned romantic poet, limping towards some inevitable doom, he felt an irresistible urge to take the piss out of this carefully invented character.

Byron's *Don Juan* is one of the great masterpieces of European literature, but he called his work 'poeshy' and said he didn't rank poetry high in the scale of intelligence. Speaking of religion, he said, 'I deny nothing, but doubt everything.' Everything, of course, included himself. No one's set of beliefs was further removed from the domino theory. You could, if you chose, call him inconsistent; but when his wife, Annabella, accused herself of inconsistency, Byron regretted he had found her guilty of no such offence and added, 'Your consistency is the most Formidable Apparition I have ever encountered.' In his own life, he was careful to avoid the Formidable Apparition, managing to combine his innate conservatism with a true love of liberty and revolutionary fervour, his romanticism with downright common sense and his puritanism with sensuality. Such potent mixtures, and contradictions, produced a more interesting character than his wife's mathematical certainties.

I once went to speak to the boys at Eton. I was in a long room which used to contain many classes in which the boys were beaten, bullied and bored by the slow, laborious recitation and translation of Virgil and Horace. The walls are decorated with the names of hundreds of dead Etonians, carved by their owners, and all in capital letters. There is, however, one name in cursive or italic script — and that is 'Shelley'. At Harrow there is an identical room, and there also all the names are in capital letters, with one exception — 'Byron'. There is no reason to think that they had ever met during their schooldays. In later life Byron found 'poor Shelley, the <u>least</u> selfish and mildest of men — a man who had made more sacrifices of his fortune and feelings for others than any I have heard of'. A remarkable testimonial, although the puritan in Byron thought it necessary to add, 'with his speculative opinions I have nothing in common, nor desire to have'. One thing they did have in common, however: they were two boys determined to be different from everyone else.

There are writers, like Oscar Wilde, whose lives are so colourful, exotic and apparently doomed that the stories they lived overshadowed the stories they invented. Byron is one of these. It's enthralling to read about his finding fame and infamy in England, his shrugging off the exhibitionist Caroline Lamb, who stalked him dressed as a pageboy, speculating about whether or not his love for his half-sister was ever consummated, following him into exile as he rattles across Europe in his coach with his doctor and his silver dinner service, to his loves and adventures in Italy.

We can picture the damp, dark ground floor of the Palazzo Mocenigo, where Byron stored his carriages and his menagerie of dogs, birds and monkeys, which included the alarming Swiss mastiff Mutz, who once turned tail and ran to avoid the attack of a pig in the Apennines. We can see him among the 'gloomy gaiety of the gondolas on the silent canals'. Following the accounts of this exotic life, we may easily forget Byron's strong belief in freedom and social justice.

The jobs of the stocking weavers of Nottingham, in Byron's home county, were threatened by the introduction of new frames, that would increase production and reduce the number of workers needed. In fact the new frames produced shoddier and less marketable stockings. Their introduction was welcomed by the employers and cursed by the workers, who, facing unemployment, responded by breaking the new machinery in a Luddite rage and occasionally rioting. A Tory government introduced a bill which would punish such irresponsible behaviour with the sentence of death.

On 27 February 1812, before he awoke to find himself famous and when *Childe*

Harold was still in the press, Byron rose in the House of Lords to oppose this measure in a speech that achieved Dickensian heights of irony and anger. The frame breakers, he said, were men convicted 'on the clearest evidence, of the capital crime of Poverty; men, who had been nefariously guilty of lawfully begetting several children, whom, thanks to the times, they were unable to maintain. Considerable injury has been done to the proprietors of the improved Frames. These machines were to them an advantage, inasmuch as they superseded the necessity of employing a number of workmen, who were left in consequence to starve.'

Dealing with this horrific imposition of the death penalty, he said, 'Is there not blood enough upon your penal code, that more must be poured forth to ascend to Heaven and testify against you? How will you carry the Bill into effect? Can you commit a whole country to their own prisons? Will you erect a gibbet in every field . . . Place the country under martial law? Depopulate and lay waste all around you? And restore Sherwood Forest as . . . an asylum for outlaws?'

At the end of his speech, he described the only sort of court likely to hang a frame breaker: 'there are two things wanting to convict and condemn him; and these are, in my opinion, — Twelve Butchers for a jury, and a Jeffries for a judge!'

This superb speech has been criticized as an 'overwrought vision of a nation reduced to political anarchy'. Lord Holland thought it 'too full of fancy', although Byron, 'having put the Lord Chancellor very much out of humour' (still a worthwhile thing to do), was glowing with success. His critics seem to have regarded the Tory bill as some more or less harmless addition to the criminal law. The outrageous nature of the proposal called for all the rhetorical weapons available in a great poet's armoury.

A week after this speech *Childe Harold* was published and on 21 April in the same year he was on his feet again, speaking in favour of Catholic emancipation in Ireland. Catholics were not allowed to become sheriffs who appointed jurors, with the result that an all-Protestant jury acquitted a Protestant when three 'reliable and respectable witnesses saw him load, take aim, fire at, and kill' a Catholic. He also pointed out that had the Irish Duke of Wellington been a Catholic, he would never have been allowed to command an army or even rise from the ranks.

He also spoke in favour of a petition to reform the ludicrous and corrupt electoral system presented by a certain Major Cartwright. Typically, the Whigs, alleged to be the more liberal party, had, in the manner of politicians, failed to support these sensible proposals and Byron was a lonely and brave voice, encouraged only by an elderly earl who was unpopularly in favour of the French Revolution. When Byron told his friend Moore about it he said, 'in a mock heroic voice', that he had been delivering a speech that was a 'most flagrant violation of the Constitution'. When Moore asked him what it was about, he seemed to have forgotten. As his most recent biographer, Fiona MacCarthy, here fairly says, the things he cared most about (poetry, love and liberal causes) he spoke of with 'a throwaway response', or even the greatest frivolity.

His short life ended dramatically in the battle to free 'the Isles of Greece' from Turkish tyranny. This grand gesture had its moments of absurdity, as when Achilles-style helmets were ordered from a hatters in Piccadilly, but there's no reason to doubt the genuineness of his attachment to the cause, which bore some resemblance to the Spanish Civil War of my childhood. This struggle was romantic and seemed, from a distance, to be morally clear: the good against the bad, the noble Greeks, inheritors of an ancient democracy, against the Fascist equivalent, cruel and authoritarian Turks. There was even an International Brigade composed of idealistic European liberals, paid for by Byron.

He arrived with high hopes, having spent £4,000 on a Greek fleet to sail to Missolonghi. He took with him Pietro Gamba, the brother of his mistress, Teresa Guiccioli, who was 'hot for revolution'. He was much taken with the warlike appearance of the Greek soldiers, the Suliotes, of whom he expected great things. As with any war fought for an ideal, it was not long before disillusion set in.

Missolonghi was a wretched place, waterlogged, evil-smelling, a breeding ground for mosquitoes and disease. There were misunderstandings with the London Committee, money was short and Byron spent a fortune of his own. The forces of freedom in Greece were divided into rival groups, each plotting against the other. In too many instances, the freedom fighters behaved no better than their oppressors, raping women, dashing Turkish brains out

93

against brick walls and massacring prisoners. Even Pietro Gamba spent a huge amount of money on a sky-blue uniform with expensive accessories. 'This comes of letting boys play the man,' Byron wrote; 'all his patriotism diminishes into the desert for a sky blue uniform.'

Worst of all, the fine Suliote soldiers, on whom he had pinned such high hopes, proved totally unreliable. They quarrelled endlessly, refused to attack Lepanto, as Byron had planned, and fought with the International Brigade so violently that a Swedish officer was stabbed and killed by a Suliote soldier. As a result of this, a number of British artificers threatened to return to England.

'Having tried in vain at every expense and considerable trouble and some danger to unite the Suliotes,' Byron wrote, 'for the good of Greece and their own — I have come to the following conclusion — I will have nothing more to do with the Suliotes. They may go to the Turks, or the Devil, — they may cut me into more pieces than they have dissensions among themselves, — sooner than change my resolution.' He had found, like many of those who have struggled for great liberal and liberating causes and beliefs, that the difficulty isn't so much fighting the enemy as stopping your friends murdering each other.

In the foul-smelling, muddy swamps of Missolonghi, Byron took a fever, had a stroke and lay, at times, unconscious. The doctors, who recommended merciless bleeding and fastened a leech to his forehead, hastened his death. His heroism lay in his ceaseless attempts to heal differences, to prevent atrocities so far as he could, to keep his temper and to retain his belief in the justice of the cause.

He was not entirely disillusioned. Freedom would still be a glorious thing, even if the heroes of the resistance turned out to be dubious and self-seeking. 'Whoever goes into Greece at presents,' he wrote in his journal, 'should do it as Mrs Fry went into Newgate [Prison] — not in the expectation of meeting with any special indication of existing probity, but in the hope that time and better treatment will reclaim the burglarious and larcenous tendencies which have followed this General Gaol delivery.'

This is excellent advice to all those anxious to join liberal, freedom-seeking, left-wing movements. Go among your fellow protesters in the merciful spirit of a prison visitor, because you are likely to meet some extremely doubtful fish.

11

Lying

Michel, Lord of Montaigne, was always a reasonable and tolerant man, but he was particularly hard on liars. 'An accursed vice,' he wrote. 'It is only our words which bind us together and make us human. If we realized the weight and horror of lying, we would see that it is more worthy of the stake than other crimes.'

A kindlier but anonymous commentator coupled two biblical pronouncements to describe lying as 'an abomination unto the Lord, but a very present help in time of trouble'. Like many other things, a lie can be a serious crime, a source of evil, a forgivable vanity or an act of mercy. Lies can be used to brighten an otherwise bleak and underpopulated life. They often reveal more about the liar than what emerges when he or she is telling the truth.

A writer of fiction must have a confused view of the truth. To a novelist the whole world is potential fiction. But leaving the peculiar question of a writer's attitude aside for a moment, what can I say that will be of any use to my inheritors about telling the truth and the occasional use of kindly deception?

In my childhood I lied very early to make my life sound more interesting. I was really the son of Russian aristocrats, smuggled out of the country after the revolution and hidden in a trunk on the Trans-Siberian Railway. The barrister and his wife who took me in were not my parents, but a kindly couple who cared for me after my true mother and father had been shot in Siberia. Whenever I began to lose faith in the likelihood of this story I dropped hints about my mother's infidelity, my parents' forthcoming divorce and the fact, which I thought would be more interesting than the dull reality, that I was about to become the child of a broken home. This invention was soon detected by those friends I took home for lunch on Sundays, who saw my parents still irritatingly devoted. I suppose I thought these and other lies about myself were necessary to brighten the dull plod through school and lonely holidays. At least they led to a determination to make life more interesting than my childhood inventions.

There may be something curiously creative about those who cling to childhood fantasies in adult life, and invent wartime adventures, perilous escapes or legendary love affairs to keep boredom at bay. One such was certainly Jeffrey Archer, Lord Archer of Weston-super-Mare, of whom my friend Ned Sherrin said, 'He was the only seaside pier [peer] not to have been performed on by the transvestite comedian Danny La Rue.' He wrote novels and took up politics, becoming the Chairman of the Conservative Party, but his greatest work of fiction may have been his life. He invented his education, his sporting achievements and much else about himself, and, I'm sure, enjoyed the results. When I was connected with the Howard League for Penal Reform, we held a drinks party on the terrace of the House of Lords for the purpose of raising money from the great and the good. Jeffrey Archer kindly came down to say a few words to the assembled company. 'Thirty years ago,' he began, 'I was having lunch with John Mortimer in a London club and John told me to join the Howard League, which I did and I have never regretted it.' This was kindly intended and produced a few cheques. The only trouble with it was that I have never had lunch with Jeffrey Archer in a London club or anywhere else. It was a small and no doubt irrelevant lie, but the truth didn't come naturally to him.

Unfortunately, Jeffrey Archer applied his talent for invention to a libel case he was involved in. I saw him last in the Old Bailey, a small, still cheerful figure peering over the edge of the dock. 'It's an honour to see you at my trial,' he said and added, 'What are you doing for lunch?' Sadly I never joined him at 'the little Italian place where they do a very quick meal' and he went off to serve what I thought was an unnecessarily long sentence in a prison from which he still managed to emerge for lunch.

Even Montaigne, safe in his tower from having to rely on anything as 'a present help in time of trouble', might have forgiven the small lies merely intended to cheer up or smooth the lives of close friends and casual acquaintances such as, 'You are looking well', or, 'I did think your poem was brilliant' or even, 'How beautiful you are today!' Even if they are true, you should use these compliments carefully. My wife was, as always, looking beautiful, but I made the mistake of telling her this when telephoning from America, which made even a truthful statement sound like an invention. But even if not strictly accurate, scattering these consoling words like confetti could hardly be a major crime, calling for burning at the stake.

To be convicted of being a serious liar you have to make a statement that you don't believe in or you know to be untrue. So members of the Flat Earth Society or those who, like the great Sir Arthur Conan Doyle, assure us that the dead are readily available to speak at seances and that there are fairies at the bottom of the garden, are not liars. The statements they make may be untrue but they are convinced that they are telling the truth. In fact, they are in the same position, I think, as many unreliable witnesses. Such witnesses go through details of the car crash, the course of the quarrel in the pub that led to the stabbing with the broken glass, the row at home that ended with a head coming into fatal contact with the stone around the hearth. They are convinced of the version of events most favourable to themselves and become sure that it must be the truth.

It's for this reason that false witnesses in court can sound so convincing. Appeal courts often defer to trial judges, who, they say, 'have seen the witnesses and can form a view as to their credibility'. Often seeing a witness is a poor, even a misleading guide. The worst liars may remember to wear ties and suits, speak considerately in time with the judge's pencil, call him 'My Lord' and survive a scorching cross-examination. Those who stammer, contradict themselves, take offence at hostile questions and come to court looking like an unmade bed can often be telling nothing but the truth.

So what of the advocate who has to stand up in court and repeat a quite possibly untrue account of events? Is he saying something he doesn't believe to be true? Quite possibly; but the advocate has gone through a process well known to those struggling for religious faith, the suspension of disbelief. My own disbelief was kept hanging up in the robing room of the Old Bailey for years. A barrister's job is to put the case for the defence as effectively and clearly as would his client if he had an advocate's skills. The barrister's belief or disbelief in the truth of this story is irrelevant: it's for the jury to decide this often difficult question. Would this explanation of a barrister's role defend him from the strict judgement of Montaigne? I know that most non-lawyers find it hard to understand and their most frequent question is, 'How can you defend a man you know to be guilty?' The answer is that if he tells you he's guilty, you can't call him to tell a story you know to be untrue. But if he says he didn't do it, you must put his case. You are a mouthpiece, a spokesman in an argument which is directed not at uncovering the truth, but at deciding whether or not the prosecution has proved guilt beyond reasonable doubt.

Life as a mouthpiece for more or less convincing stories can, in the end, prove unsatisfactory. For the writer the situation is entirely different. For him, falsehood is not a thing which has to be decided by other people. He is no longer a stand-in for anyone else. He must look into himself and find the particular truth which is his alone and be faithful to it in all that he writes. He must express a view of the world which seems truthful to him, regardless of what anybody else may think about it. So although it may seem odd, the person whose trade has least to do with lying is not the lawyer or the businessman or, most certainly, the politician. It's the writer of fiction.

12

The Companionship of Women

This section is intended for those of my heirs and assigns as happen to be men. Men are undoubtedly going through a hard time nowadays. It's not such a hard time as women went through when they couldn't own property or divorce their husbands for adultery and felt compelled to publish their novels under assumed masculine names. In divorce cases they could be valued in cash terms, as though they were so much real estate, and if they found their husbands no longer sexually attractive they could be met with a legal proceeding known as a Petition for Restitution of Conjugal Rights (Restitution of Convivial Nights, the old hands in the Probate, Divorce and Admiralty Division used to call it). If the conjugal rights were not forthcoming a hard-up and estranged husband could claim maintenance from his rich, lawfully wedded wife on the grounds of her 'wilful refusal' of sex.

Men may never be the victims of such absurd acts of subjugation. Their difficulties are more subtle but, none the less, real. Boys at school are easily outdistanced by girls, who take their lessons more seriously and are not, on the whole, proud of failure. Women are more realistic and open-minded than men, who tend to live in a world of wishful thinking, fantasy and make-believe. For that reason I always welcomed women on juries, although the old-fashioned criminals I defended thought that a woman's place was in the kitchen, or looking after the children, and not out robbing banks or sitting in judgement on hard-working safe breakers and those accused of long-firm fraud.

I'm conscious of the fact that all that I have just written is sexist, politically incorrect, oversimplified and grossly unfair to the male sex. Male and female characteristics are not evenly distributed to men and women. Quite apart from homosexual preferences, there are men with strong female perceptions and women with a masculine tendency to self-delusion. But I suppose the reasons for most women's realistic attitude to life lie in the physical changes she has to suffer. Bleeding and stopping bleeding and coping with the agony of childbirth are traumas such as no man has to suffer. His only certain suffering is death, thoughts of which can, even in old age, be postponed indefinitely. Forcing a living, breathing human being out of your body is an encounter with reality from which men find themselves thankfully absolved. It's hard enough for us to pluck up the courage to be in the room when this alarming process is taking place.

Perhaps it's having gone to an all-boys school that made me for the rest of my life prefer the company of women. Homosexuality seemed to be the only choice on offer in my schooldays. We scarcely saw a woman, there were no female teachers and our meals were served by two footmen in blue coats with gold buttons (they frequently cut themselves shaving and would bleed in the cabbage) and a butler in tails. The boys, when not involved in sexual approaches to each other, seemed greatly interested in sport, which included a strange version of football played with a ball shaped like a cheese and, from time to time, the throwing of a stick on to the ground with a strange cry of 'Yards!'

Sometimes games and sex became curiously involved. One of the butlers was said to conceal himself behind a bush on the way to the games fields. He would then covertly change his tailcoat for football clothing and trot down to join in the rugby scrum. This gave him ample opportunity to interfere with the boys. Brought up in this atmosphere, I rapidly became allergic to any game which involved chasing a ball up and down a muddy field in a fine drizzle. I have to confess that this reluctance to participate has spread to all games, even those such as contract bridge and backgammon, during which there is little danger from partially disguised butlers out for sex.

It has also confirmed my belief that hell would be an eternal masculine public-school reunion, or a black-tie dinner of all-male chartered accountants. When Yeats wrote his poem, and made his will, he included 'Memories of the words of women' as part of the recipe for a 'superhuman, mirror-resembling dream'. The words of men in the locker room or down the pub during a boys' night out are not of such a superhuman dream-like quality.

And, in spite of David and Jonathan, Hamlet and Horatio, Caesar and Antony, Bush and Blair, women have a greater gift, I think, for friendship. It's true that girls in school can be extraordinarily bitchy to each other; but both at school and in after-life they are capable of forming great networks of friends to spread news and gossip and cheerfully discover the inadequacies of their husbands. The air between mobile phones is heavy with the words of women confiding in each other — and of men failing to communicate.

So it is always better to sit in a restaurant with a woman. Fantasies can wander freely over the creamed spinach and Dover sole. There are always vague possibilities hovering over the table, however young or old the couple. Perhaps it's more restful if they have been lovers in the past, if that is over and done with and perhaps seems, in retrospect, even better than it was at the time. If they are very old and not quite sure whether it happened or not, it's better to assume that it did and speak with the appropriate nostalgic yearning for the past. Whatever the relationship was, is or might have been, you can be sure that women will drink as much and smoke more vehemently between courses than men; but they will be more full of shared secrets, astute observations, anecdotes to be treasured and opinions to be expounded than men at a restaurant table. You are soon lulled into the belief that you are the only person in the world they would ever say half of these things to.

Looking back down the long corridor of the years, you will be able to remember so many glorious women and wonder why it is that so many of them have married such appalling husbands. Robert Graves wrote a poem on this subject and ended with a thought I share:

> *Or do I always over-value woman*
> *At the expense of man?*
> *Do I?*
> *It might be so.*

13

Causing Offence

Causing offence, together with smoking, fox-hunting and the enjoyment of a motor-car, is now considered criminal conduct by the politically correct. This is a serious mistake. A life during which you're caused no offence would be as blandly uneventful as death itself. Being caused offence stirs up the spirits, summons up the blood and starts the adrenalin flowing. A parliamentary system that includes an official opposition and an adversarial method of trial proves the effectiveness of going on the offensive to reach the truth. A state in which everyone tiptoed around whispering for fear of hurting somebody's feelings would be dull beyond human endurance. A political or religious belief which can't stand up to insult, mockery and abuse is not worth having.

The sad signs are, however, that anxiety about causing offence has reached the point of insanity. A town council was censured recently for advertising a job for candidates with 'pleasing personalities'. This was objected to as it might cause offence to people with displeasing personalities. The three towering geniuses of European culture, Shakespeare, Mozart and Leonardo da Vinci, were not allowed to appear on the euro note as they might, in their separate ways, cause offence: Mozart because he was a 'womanizer', Shakespeare because he wrote *The Merchant of Venice*, a play judged to be anti-Semitic, and Leonardo because he was reported to fancy boys. Now the euro note carries a picture of a rather dull bridge.

The urge to ban words which might possibly cause offence has now become surreal. The sublime works of P.G. Wodehouse describe many decent and dependable characters, some being members of the Drones Club, as 'good eggs'. You would think this would be praise everyone would value. I remember doing an interview with Raquel Welch, whom I found, rather to my surprise, to be an 'excellent egg'. When I wrote that, there were no cries of protest, the beautiful actress in question appeared to regard it as a compliment, and I was not aware of having caused offence to anyone.

Now, however, it appears that a police officer calling anyone a good or indeed any sort of egg would be strictly reprimanded. Why on earth should that be? You may well ask. Of course, the answer is extremely simple. 'Egg and spoon' is cockney rhyming slang for 'coon' and so 'egg' is a word of racial abuse, isn't it? Or is it? Partridge's dictionary of slang gives no authority for the egg and spoon theory, and there must be many to whom this involved connection would never occur. However, in the world we live in, this is no doubt an excellent reason for keeping P.G. Wodehouse's face off the euro note.

Sensitive police officers were also deeply concerned when a Home Office minister urged them to get down to the 'nitty-gritty' of a certain problem. You will have realized at once why this is a term of racist abuse and likely to give terrible offence. The Home Office minister, it seems, was ignorant of what every trainee constable knows: the bilges at the bottom of slave ships were where the dirty water sloshed around the grit from the ballast. Any reference to this area, where slaves were once kept in chains, would naturally be deeply offensive to a law student from Ghana or a young doctor from Sierra Leone. Or would it? Referring once more to the great Partridge, you will find that the expression 'nitty-gritty' has its origins among the black musicians in New York in the 1930s, a time when very few slave ships were crossing the Atlantic. And even if it did have to do with the ghastly trade in human beings, what's wrong with using the words to describe the unpleasant basic reality of a problem?

But the desperate need to find words which might, just possibly, offend someone requires no logic or even a working knowledge of the language. The university teacher in America who used the word 'niggardly' knew that it had absolutely nothing to do with the colour of anyone's skin, but apparently his audience and the university authorities didn't. So he lost his job.

If you are English and say you don't mind at all being called a 'whingeing Pom' in Australia, if you are Scots and are not in the least offended by jokes about your being careful with your money, you are told that it's perfectly all right for those who are so secure, so complacent, so self-satisfied that they can even take a bit of offence without serious danger. But the idea that there are other, weaker, more easily offended people who may go into a decline if told that they are, after all, good eggs seems to me intolerably patronizing.

The fact that words are held in such awe is no doubt flattering to writers. We are dealing in goods which are thought of as being as deadly as bullets, as destructive as Exocet missiles. In the beginning was the word. This is one of the comparatively rare moments when I find myself in complete agreement with God. In fact the word, in the Old Testament, *is* God. Words can be used for some of His most terrible purposes, for starting wars, for pronouncing death sentences on criminals and cancer sufferers, for inciting rebellions and ordering hideous reprisals, for announcing great and poetic truths and for lying and deceit. No one can deny their power and, with all respect to Dr Dolittle, they are what separate us from the animals. But how far should the use of words be a criminal offence? Threats to kill, conspiracies to murder or to rob, incitements to violence, even, under more sensible libel laws than those we have in England at present, perhaps untrue or unjustified accusations of bad behaviour that cause financial loss must be against the law. But, for heaven's sake, words that give offence, as indeed the word of God has down the ages to many people, are an essential part of life.

'Have you heard the argument? Is there no offence in't?' the guilty King asks Hamlet as the Players start to reenact his crime. 'No offence i' the world,' Hamlet lies, and it's as well that he does. A play with no offence in it would make a dull evening in any theatre. Indeed, it might be said that the arts advanced on a tide of offence. The Puritans in the times of Cromwell, true ancestors of the politically correct, found the glory of the Elizabethan and Jacobean dramatists so offensive that they closed the theatres and acting was made a criminal offence punishable by flogging. Satirists from Juvenal to Pope and onwards handed out strong doses of offence, often in exquisite couplets. Shelley's *Queen Mab* was considered so offensive that its printer was put on trial for blasphemy. Byron, writing 'God Save the King / It is a small economy' on the death of George III, was as offensive about the monarch, and such popular heroes as the Duke of Wellington, as *Private Eye* manages to be today. *Madame Bovary* was thought so offensive that Flaubert was put on trial for it, as was Baudelaire for *Les*

Fleurs du Mal. Ibsen's *Ghosts* offended by dealing with hereditary syphilis, and in my lifetime *Ulysses, Lady Chatterley's Lover* and *The Well of Loneliness* were all banned. Arthur Miller's *A View from the Bridge*, in which men kissed, and John Osborne's *A Patriot for Me* couldn't be played unless the theatres were, for some archaic legal reason, turned into clubs. It was feared that they might offend the public at large. In painting, Whistler's river views deeply offended Ruskin. Practically everyone was hugely offended by the first Impressionist exhibition and the Surrealists caused even more offence than pickled cows or Tracey Emin's bed.

It is true to say that Mrs Radclyffe Hall's story of lesbian love, *The Well of Loneliness*, having been clearly found unfit for human consumption by a London Police Court magistrate in the 1930s, was a few years ago read aloud on BBC Radio as the 'Book at Bedtime'. Fashions in what is or is not offensive change over the years and it might even be said that the present standards of sensitivity are sillier than ever. You can understand, even if you don't agree with, public discomfort about an open discussion of hereditary syphilis or lesbian love. It's harder to believe that any sane person could be seriously concerned about good eggs or getting down to the nitty-gritty.

The most serious offence, it once was thought, would be caused if free speech were to be allowed on the subject of religious beliefs. Living in a country where we assumed speech to be free, it was something of a shock to discover that we still had a blasphemy law that, in true medieval fashion, made offensive remarks about religion a crime. In the 1930s a Mr Gough was sent to prison for suggesting that Christ looked like a clown when he rode into Jerusalem on a donkey. In the 1970s James Kirkup wrote a poem describing the Roman centurion's physical desire for the dead body of Christ when He was taken down from the cross. This poem was published in the magazine *Gay News*. The editor of that paper was convicted of blasphemy and sentenced to a term of imprisonment. Although the prison sentence was quashed on appeal, the surprising fact remained that we had a blasphemy law which protects only the Church of England (you can say what you like about the Pope) and no other religion. The inevitable result of this was that other religious groups wanted one too and a Labour Home Secretary, who is to civil liberties what terriers are to rats, was on the point of making it a crime to cause offence to anyone's religious belief, until good sense and the House of Lords spared us, for the moment, any such legislation. Another result was that those who defended the fatwah, the death sentence passed in Iran against Salman Rushdie because of what he had written about the prophet Mohammed, were able to tell us that we have a law against blasphemy so how could we criticize Islamic fundamentalists?

It is surely absurd to believe that Christians, who have survived persecution, martyrdom and generations of religious wars, would crumble at a few words of mockery, criticism or even abuse. It seems to me to be an insult to the religious beliefs, as well as to those who hold them, to say that they need the special protection of a law which makes it a criminal offence to hurt people's feelings.

When the jury was out in the *Gay News* trial, Mrs Whitehouse, the litigious leader of the National Viewers' and Listeners' Association, prayed with her supporters in the corridors of the Old Bailey for a guilty verdict. In his autobiography the judge revealed that he felt the hand of God writing his summing-up. If this were so, God has defined our blasphemy law as one having no requirement of intent (you needn't *mean* to upset any one) and one without any defence of literary merit. The Almighty has clearly changed his mind since the more liberal days when *On the Origin of Species* was published and 'intent' was said to be a vital part of the offence. No one wanted to put Darwin in the nick.

Writers and artists must learn to withstand mockery, abuse and misunderstanding as an essential part of their careers. Men and women of various political beliefs, however sincerely held, must expect derision. It seems very strange that the Church of England, often seen as among the gentler religions, should wish to be protected by a censor or find it necessary to combine its beliefs with the threat of imprisonment.

In fact being caused offence not only stimulates debate but confirms belief and strengthens it. Milton, no enemy of religion, had it right when he wrote 'if we have free speech truth will look after itself'. And if we have a censorship which stops us offending anyone, the truth may be concealed in the surrounding blur.

14

Living with Children

When I think of my childhood it smells of bracken. The common near which we lived was covered with the stuff — crisp, brown and crackling in the winter, green and sticky with sap in the summer. In this bracken Sam Rockall, Iris and I would, build houses, rescue broken plates and cups from the nearest rubbish dump, drink Tizer the Appetizer and consume jam sandwiches, gob-stoppers and bags of crisps that always contained, in those days, a little blue bag of salt. Sam Rockall's father was a bodger, a person who cut down the beech trees, turned them into chair legs on a foot lathe and then sold them, for a few pounds a gross, to the furniture makers in High Wycombe.

So every day during my school holidays, we played together, often staying out until the sun went down and the glow-worms shone on the common. Then we went home to what Sam and Iris called tea and my parents called dinner. Although, from time to time, Iris would volunteer to show me her knickers and I occasionally presented her with a Woolworth's necklace, our activities were entirely innocent.

Often I bicycled seven miles to the river at Henley and swam in the dark, brackish waters where your feet tangled in the rushes or sank into the riverbed so that the mud oozed between your toes. No one swims in the river now — a pity, because in spite of its being the receptacle into which the lavatories of pleasure boats are emptied, it had a good deal more interest than a chlorinated swimming pool.

So I bicycled, and talked to strangers — a slightly mad monk and an artist I found doing a painting of Henley Bridge. I don't think my parents worried very much, or wondered where I was. Perhaps they were relieved at my absence. When I was at home, I would perform scenes from my favourite musical films and, having no brother or sister, I had to be both Fred Astaire and Ginger Rogers. Having a child in those days didn't seem to be a matter of perpetual anxiety.

Even at my prep school we were allowed to bicycle round Oxford to buy fruit and materials to assemble model aeroplanes or, in my case, copies of *Theatre World.* My parents used to treat me with mild amusement and I don't remember being put under any pressure to pass exams. The freedom, some people nowadays might even call it the neglect, of a 1930s childhood was a good preparation for an uncertain future. When I was sixteen war broke out and from the heights of Harrow churchyard we could see the sky coloured red as London burned. There could be no further guarantee of safety.

Childhood now seems a far more sheltered, even claustrophobic, period of life. Television and the Internet are mechanical devices that have taken the place of imaginary adventures, when you could be a captain in the French Foreign Legion galloping to relieve a fortress in the desert, or an outlaw desperate to reach his hideout in the woods.

There was no television in my childhood, of course, but we had radio, with *ITMA, In Town Tonight* and *Dick Barton, Special Agent.* But radio is a form that does call for an act of the imagination; the world is not presented to you in small, bright pictures or in flickering letters on a screen.

All these mechanical aids mean staying indoors. You can lie in the long grass or on a beach with a book but the telly has to be plugged in, in a room. And children today get driven to school (if middle class and living in London in large and inappropriate four-wheel drives) and back. If the children were out leading imaginary charges, or hiding in the bracken for fear of arrest by the King's officers, today's parents would be consumed with anxiety.

To some extent this is understandable. We live, it seems, in the age of paedophilia. The onset of this undoubted danger is a mystery to me. At boarding school we had the odd errant butler and some over-affectionate masters, but no one thought of the danger of being dragged into a strange car and ending up, perhaps dead, in the bracken.

In the 1950s and 1960s I did a large number of divorce cases. Warring wives would make the most terrible allegations against their husbands, but I can't remember any charge of paedophilia. Now practically every case in the Family Division contains such accusations. They are, of course, easy to make and are apparently included as a matter of course in American matrimonial cases. Should we believe that this horror emerged, like sex, at the time of the Beatles' first LP and grew with the encouragement of the Internet? Whatever the answer to these questions, parents have the right to be nervous. But we can't let the worst cases, however horrible, overshadow our children's lives.

Childhood, after all, has to be an age of discovery. These are days you'll remember vividly all your life, even when you're old and forget why you came into a room. It must never be allowed to become the age of anxiety.

The anxiety has been greatly increased by this government's multiplication of exams and emphasis on starting training as a middle manager in a computer company from the age of six. Parents have made things worse by worrying unduly about exam results and seeing that their children work a great deal harder than most middle managers in computer companies. During a career as a barrister, and as a writer in a number of different forms, I have to say that no one has ever asked me how I did in any school exams, or what kind of degree I got.

Our present Minister of Education has said, in a phrase that proclaims his total unsuitability for the post, that no one should study classics or medieval history and that education unconnected with qualifications for a job is 'dodgy'. This is dangerous rubbish. Childhood is the time when you should enrich your life, learn poetry, be thrilled by history, do plays, go to the cinema and look at pictures. The qualifications for a job, such as, for example, Minister of Education, can be picked up quite easily later in life.

Childhood, you should remember, is a pretty tough time to be alive. You reach, at first, only as high as grownup people's knees and then to their crotches. For this reason, you are not often referred to or included in the conversation. Sometimes you are spoken of as though you weren't there, or, if there, incapable of speaking for yourself. Strange, hairy people with patronizing smiles and penetrating voices will ask each other, 'Does he like his school?' or 'Is he enjoying his cricket? All boys like cricket.' Down at crotch level you know it's not worth saying you hate your bloody school and cricket is about as interesting an occupation as watching paint dry. You were a boy and although you were only truly excited by the plays of Noël Coward, the lyrics of Cole Porter and Jerome Kern, the seemingly casual, elegant, incredibly skilled tap-dancing of Fred Astaire, cricket is what boys like.

This, anyway, was my experience of childhood. But my parents, although they may have laughed gently at my eccentricities, didn't patronize me. When they went out to dinner or to the theatre they took me with them and there was very little talk of cricket. All the same, I was sent away to schools ruled, as much as anything, by fear. Some of the masters treated us with undisguised contempt. 'Revolting boy,' a pallid and supercilious French teacher would snort. 'Convey my sympathy to your unfortunate parents.' The masters we loved were Mr Retty (Rats), who taught us to foxtrot and, taking the woman's position on the parquet, would issue such gentle commands as, 'Chassé, boy! Please do chassé.' And Mr Jacques, who would sing to us, accompanying himself on a banjo, such songs as 'The Captain's name was Captain Brown and he played his ukulele as the ship went down' and 'Your baby has gone down the plughole'.

Children are extremely resilient and can somehow brave the fear-ridden schools of the past and the overprotection, overtesting exam mania and paedophilia obsession of today (Mr Rats would be instantly dismissed for taking the woman's part when fox-trotting with us, his arm around our waists). The only advice I can give to my heirs and assigns is to beseech them to treat children as equals: don't patronize them or ignore them or behave as though they were in some way disabled and not entirely sane.

It is also advisable to arrange your life so that you always have a young child living with you. If this, as the years go by, becomes increasingly difficult, borrow as many children as possible from the neighbours and try as hard as you can not to earn their contempt. Children can spot pomposity, insincerity and self-regard a mile off and are the best possible antidote to such diseases. They should always be heard, but they may not be seen. Let's hope they are up a tree somewhere, reading a book that has nothing to do with getting a job.

15

Interesting Times

According to a Chinese proverb, you should avoid 'interesting times', a piece of advice I would endorse. The trouble is that the world is never at peace, and interesting times interrupt most lives more or less disastrously.

I was born only five years after the 1914–18 war ended and at my prep school we drew pictures of soldiers with tin hats and bloodstained bandages, graves in fields of poppies with Camel and Fokker aeroplanes machine-gunning each other in the sky. At the Armistice Day services on the football field we sang 'Lest we forget' and an ex-army padre would urge us to go 'over the top' to our common entrance exams and school certificates. Our masters still suffered from shell shock and battle fatigue and some had pieces of shrapnel lodged in their bodies, a fact which didn't improve their tempers.

By the time I was sixteen another war had started, an event that we had long been expecting. We had heard the hysterical speeches of Hitler on the wireless and discovered that he was making yet another final demand. At one moment a senior master came into the classroom and told us that our Prime Minister had met Hitler in Munich and 'peace in our time was assured'. After that, watching the news reels that tempered my delight in the latest Fred Astaire–Ginger Rogers musical film, I felt sure of war in my time. I still believed that the odds on my survival were better than those against soldiers in the first war, who had a one-in-four chance only of lasting beyond the first months in the trenches.

When I discussed my future with my father and I was finding it hard to choose between becoming a conscientious objector or a fighter pilot, he told me to 'avoid the temptation to do anything heroic'. This was advice I took and, after bombs started falling in London, I became, as a result of various shadows about the lungs, a scriptwriter in uniform, writing propaganda (we called them documentary) films about the progress of the war for the Ministry of Information. It's true that I was doing nothing much more heroic than fire-watching on the roof of Pinewood Studios. In the morning the streets were full of broken glass. In spite of all this the time of war contains some of the happiest years I can remember. This may seem a shameful thing to admit to in a period of unparalleled horror, genocide and the destruction of entire cities, but it's true. I'm sure that during the great disasters of history, the Hundred Years War, the Black Death, the Reign of Terror or the Battle of the Somme, there were people, somewhere, quite enjoying themselves. It's not a thing to be particularly proud of.

So, drinking with Dylan Thomas and the Scottish painters Colquhoun and MacBryde in the Swiss Pub in Soho, going without bananas, eating strange food — whale steak ('Moby Dick and Chips') — and being so hard pressed for alcohol that communion wine, sometimes qualified with spirits (gin and altars), occasionally appeared at parties. I was falling in and out of love and living in the house of the owner of a contraceptive shop who blew up her wares and painted them jolly colours to serve as balloons at Christmas. All this seemed part of a normal and normally happy youth.

Our situation then cannot be compared

to the wantonly cruel attack on the twin towers in New York. No comparisons can possibly diminish the horror of that event. Although the Blitz may have scored as many deaths in a week as the American tragedy in a day, we were in a war and death from the air was, in those years, an everyday occurrence. New York, unlike London and Berlin, has never been the object of bombardment or occupied by an enemy, like Paris or Rome. All the same, it's worth thinking for a moment about morality in times of war and the reality of a projected 'war against terrorism'.

The Second World War seemed undoubtedly just. If we had lost it millions more innocent people would have been murdered in gas chambers, freedom would have become a criminal offence and there would have been a triumph of evil. The good were our allies: the Russians, who suffered huge casualties in the war against Hitler; the Americans, who for the second time came to the rescue of Europe; and, of course, the freedom fighters. All over Europe the defeated countries were heroically and secretly carrying on the fight. These rebels would, I suppose, have been called 'terrorists' by their occupying masters, who would torture and kill them, together with many innocent civilians, after every act of subversion. To us they were not just 'freedom fighters' but heroes, or in many cases heroines, of the resistance. Some time ago I was talking to an elderly woman in the South of France. When she was no more than a schoolgirl in the occupied zone, she wanted to join the local resistance group. In order to qualify for entry, she had to have shot at least one German officer. So she pedalled around with a loaded revolver in the basket on her handlebars. The first officer she saw had grey hair and looked rather like her uncle, so she couldn't shoot him. The next was sitting on a fallen tree reading a book, an attitude she found appealing, so he was spared. The third, wearing a moustache and out for a run, had nothing particularly attractive about him, so she shot and killed him and was able to join the group.

She didn't tell me more about her underground activities, but had she lobbed a bomb into a café which contained a handful of enemy officers and their girlfriends, together with a number of innocent customers, and blown up the lot of them, she would still have been greeted as a heroine of the resistance, which, to us, she undoubtedly was.

Most people in the West, certainly everyone in Israel, would agree that the Palestinian suicide bombers, who kill women and children, are terrorists. Not many people remember when Palestine, as the land of Israel was once called, was in that obscure state, a British Protectorate. Were the Jewish members of the Stern Gang, those who hanged a British sergeant with piano wire or organized the bomb in the King David Hotel with murderous results (the organization in which Prime Minister Begin started his political career), 'freedom fighters' or 'terrorists'? What, looking at the matter from an entirely neutral standpoint, would we call them now?

A terrorist, the dictionary tells us, is 'one who favours or uses terror-inspiring methods of governing or of coercing government or community'. This would certainly cover Russian activities in Chechnya and Israeli invasions into Palestinian territory, killing innocent men, women and children and even employees of the United Nations, in a prolonged attempt to fight ruthless terrorism with ruthless terrorism. The word 'terrorist' could certainly have been applied to Nelson Mandela before his trial. If it means the calculated mass killing of civilians to obtain an end, it must be applied to the destruction of Hamburg and Düsseldorf and, of course, to the dropping of H-bombs. So all these activities can be defined as 'terrorism' if they are committed by an enemy or 'freedom-fighting' if by a friend. If so, the conception of a 'war' against it calls for the most careful thought.

Of the old, violent anarchist groups it was said that they always contained one pathological killer, one selfless idealist and one police spy. It was difficult, at first glance, to tell which was which, but the idealist was always the most dangerous. A 'war against terrorism' is an impracticable conception if it means fighting terrorism with terrorism. The feelings on both sides are not that they are taking part in some evil and criminal act but risking their lives heroically for what they consider to be a just cause. You could understandably reduce terrorism by improving security and increasing the number of police spies, but it can only finally be reduced by removing the number of just causes. ANC terrorism was pointless after the end of apartheid. Terrorism in Israel will stop only when a just solution has been agreed to and the occupied territories handed back. Terrorism has existed in Ireland since Elizabeth I sent the Earl of Essex out in an unsatisfactory attempt to quell the rebels. However, since former terrorists have become government ministers in Northern Ireland, some progress has been made and sometimes the signs are hopeful. Long ago I defended a Protestant terrorist, we'll call him Ian, who was charged with gun-running under the cover of a chemist shop in Hammersmith. I remember the case vividly because of the remarkable dialogue with the police superintendent.

SUPERINTENDENT: Well, Ian, where's the gun?

IAN: Sure the only gun I've got is between my legs and it gets me into constant trouble with my wife, Noreen.

The case proceeded and Ian was given a fairly lenient term of imprisonment by an Old Bailey judge who probably favoured the Protestant cause.

Dissolve to Waterstone's bookshop in Belfast many years later. I am signing books and an extremely respectable-looking middle-aged lady in a twin set and pearls comes up and asks me to sign a book for her two sons, who are both now practising as lawyers in Northern Ireland. She also tells me that they have a very nice home near the Mountains of Mourne. Then she says suddenly and to my considerable surprise, 'Ian died ten years ago.'

'Ian?'

'Yes. Surely you remember him? You defended him about the guns run through the chemist shop in Hammersmith.'

So she was Noreen, who once gave Ian trouble about the gun between his legs.

It was only a small light at the end of one dark tunnel and it would be ridiculous to suppose that all the terrorists or the freedom fighters, whatever you call them, will end up with sons who are respectable barristers with lovely homes in the Mountains of Mourne.

Now that we have been involved in another war, causing the deaths of many innocent civilians, you may wonder if there is any such thing as a civilized way of conducting warfare. I can think only of the far-off days when Federico da Montefeltro was born, perhaps an illegitimate child, in the year Henry V of England died. Up to the age of fifteen he got an excellent education in Mantua, learning not only Latin and Greek but horsemanship, fencing, painting, music and dancing. When he inherited his dukedom, his study in the palace was lined with portraits of his heroes, including Dante and Petrarch, Homer and Virgil, Plato, Aristotle and St Augustine. He became the patron of the greatest artists of his day, Raphael and Piero della Francesca among them. When he marched out to war, musicians played and poets read their latest works aloud. All of this makes him sound entirely different from the sort of guns for hire who appear in the novels of Freddy Forsyth, though Duke Federico of Urbino was, to put it bluntly, a mercenary.

The city states of a disunited Italy were constantly at war. Florence fought Siena, Venice and Naples, and the Papal territories were either forging uneasy alliances or fighting each other. Duke Federico sold his military services to the highest bidder, but once bought he was a loyal and effective commander. No doubt his price went up when, in contemporary lists of the leaders whom young princes should try to emulate, Federico's name was mentioned along with those of Philip of Macedon, Alexander the Great and Julius Caesar. Sometimes his engagements were hard-fought battles, sometimes they seem to have been more civilized occasions. At the Battle of La Molinella, at which Federico commanded the forces of Florence and Milan against the Venetians, as neither side appeared to be winning he and the other mercenary leader decided to call the whole thing off. Machiavelli wrote of it with some contempt: 'Neither side wavered, no one fell, a few prisoners and a wounded horse being the only casualty of the encounter!'

The positive outcome of these battles, sometimes bloody, occasionally polite, was that Federico built 'on a rugged site of Urbino a palace which many believe to be the most beautiful in all Italy', according to Castiglione, the author of *The Courtier*. In an upstairs gallery hangs the most enigmatic and chilling of all small paintings, Piero della Francesca's *Flagellation*.

Piero was a great mathematician, a student of Euclid with such a perfect sense of perspective that he could draw a vase seen from four different angles at the same time. The lines of the buildings, the geometrically perfect placing of events, are mathematically satisfying — it's the subject of the picture that freezes the blood. In the distance something terrible is going on: the whipping of the near-naked Christ bound to a pillar. The men in the foreground are taking absolutely no notice of this scene.

They are talking quietly together, engrossed in some plot or political machination remote from human suffering.

Piero certainly came to Urbino and his geometry may well have had its effect on the deeply satisfying architecture at the Ducal Palace. You can stand in its courtyard and feel what a building of perfect proportions, conceived with mathematical precision on the scale of humanity, can do to banish anxiety and calm the spirit. It's undoubtedly the greatest legacy of a civilized soldier who had participated in other people's wars.

Federico died of a fever contracted on the damp and marshy banks of the Po in a battle against the Venetians and the Pope. Although he lived by selling war like takeaway pizzas, he was said to be 'known for his clemency' and entitled to be called 'the father of the miserable and protector of the afflicted'.

I was writing this in January, a refugee from an English winter, in a garden where red, yellow and white roses were in bloom and the call to prayer from the mosque in the village echoed across the orange groves. We were in the south of Morocco, where the people are gentle, smiling, anxious to please and many of them speak French. They might be regarded by the American and European tourists who are staying away as part of the Islamic hordes who threaten the very existence of our Western civilization.

We were almost alone in this hotel ten years ago during the Gulf War, and now it was once again a place of peace. Early in the morning an icy wind blew from the desert but by ten o'clock the sun had risen high over the trees and we were sitting by the pool with Roland. He was a Swiss dealer and collector of ancient coins who once had in his hands the first known money, pieces of gold stamped with the sign of King Croesus. Naturally the talk turned to Baghdad — in a country that was once called Mesopotamia, Roland remembered, the birthplace of our civilization, which spread to Egypt, Greece and Rome before being washed up on the shores of our small and distant island.

It was part of the Persian Empire, conquered by Alexander the Great, said Roland, who can track the course of history from the coins that may have changed hands in Babylon. I could remember only that the Hanging Gardens were one of the Seven Wonders of the World and a childhood nursery rhyme which gave the city a feeling of magic.

How many miles to Babylon?
Threescore miles and ten.
Can I get there by candle-light?
Yes, and back again.

'The Persian empire was conquered by Alexander the Great,' said Roland, who had seen coins to prove it. 'Then Alexander married a Persian wife and divided his empire among his generals. Much later, in the time of Charlemagne, the biggest city in the world was in Mesopotamia, called Medina al Salaam, the city of peace, later known as Baghdad. It was once so glitzy and exotic that New York was known as Baghdad on the subway.'

'Roland knows everything,' I told his wife.

'Not quite everything,' she said. She was calm and beautiful — a grandmother whose banker parents were turned out of Yugoslavia by Tito and arrived, penniless, in Geneva. 'Everything about coins and history perhaps. But not quite everything.' She slid into the pool and swam away, as expertly as a young girl, blowing out air under water.

At lunch by the flowering bougainvillea, with a view of the snowline on the Atlas Mountains, the waiters in long white djellabas moved quietly out of the shadows. We drank cold, pink Moroccan wine and Roland was on to his special subject, crusader coins, many of which had their crosses changed to crescents for use by the Arabs.

'When a crusader lost a leg,' he told us, 'his followers would put a red-hot sword on the stump and rely on God to do the rest. The Arabs already had skilled surgeons who cauterized and sewed up the wounds.

'Mesopotamia became part of the Ottoman Empire,' said Roland, continuing with history as told by the money clinking in the purses and pockets of long-lost generations. 'It was owned by the Turks. When Turkey was defeated in the 1914–18 war, the Allies carved up its possessions with quite arbitrary boundaries and placed an arbitrary king, Feisal, on the throne of Iraq. These kings ruled until a revolution led by the Baath party finally produced Saddam Hussein who was, of course, backed by America. Now politicians think we are about to fight barbaric Muslim hordes. In fact Arabs are at the centre of civilization. They invented algebra [an Arabic word], conquered almost the whole of Spain and managed to live there perfectly happily with the Sephardic Jews.'

Rashid, the young waiter who helps me to my seat by the pool and settles me down to write until lunchtime, has just got married. By a pure coincidence, his wife is Rashida, so *Rashid and Rashida* sounds like a happy opera, perhaps a little-known work by Rossini. He brought us his wedding photographs. Rashida is very young and pretty, wearing a tiara and a glittering robe for the occasion. She and Rashid gave each other ceremonial dates and sips of milk. Rashida had her hands and feet stained with henna. They knew each other in their schooldays. Rashida's mother died giving birth to her and her father left home to live in Fez with another wife. She lived with an uncle she called 'papa' and was clearly delighted to have a family of her own. Rashid, putting the wedding photographs away in a plastic bag, was also delighted. 'Goodbye, celibacy,' is what he said.

We drove through the camels and donkey carts in the back streets of Taroudannt and climbed a perilous staircase to Rashid and Rashida's spotless apartment. The biscuits and pancakes, the tea and the coffee were laid out and the television was alight with soundless cartoons. Rashid had changed out of his white djellaba and was wearing black jeans, a black zipper jacket and very dark glasses, so that he looked like a young film director of the Jean-Luc Godard era.

After tea we sat with Rashid (but without Rashida) and Mustapha the driver in the bar of the Hotel Taroudannt. This was a narrow courtyard with a long flowerbed in its centre, from which trees grew and numberless small tortoises stirred in perpetual motion. Rashid and Mustapha knew almost everyone who passed, most of them seemed to be their relations and all got a kiss, including a policeman. I was drinking pastis and feeling, for the moment, entirely happy. Then someone asked me to explain why the Americans and the British should wish to kill Arab women and children. It was a question I found difficult to answer.

Rita, the hotel's Moroccan owner, was the granddaughter of a grand vizier to the king, a man able to sit down to dinner with a different wife every day of the week. She is married to an Italian and she is one of the few Muslims to have gone through a Catholic wedding ceremony. She talked about the Sunnis and the Shias in Iraq who, sharing almost exactly the same religion, hate each other more bitterly than they hate Christians or Jews. There seems to be no greater cause for mutual loathing than sharing similar religious beliefs, so Catholic and Protestant have slaughtered each other throughout history. The end of Saddam, Rita said, will mean civil strife, anarchy and chaos.

We thought we were going to war because Saddam Hussein refused to reveal the existence, or non-existence, of 'weapons of mass destruction'. Had he done so, it seemed, he would have been allowed to go on tyrannizing in peace. Then the story changed and we were going to fight him anyway, and for the more persuasive reason that Iraq was ruled by terror, torture and mass executions. Perhaps wars don't happen for logical or even readily understandable reasons. Who remembers in what war, for what just or unjust cause, the charge of the Light Brigade was blunderingly launched? Who can disinter, with any accuracy, the causes of the 1914–18 war, in which millions marched cheerfully to their deaths? What exactly were the decimated regiment of the Gloucesters up to in Korea? What was the point of the long-drawn-out death, destruction and demoralization of the unsuccessful American war in Vietnam? Do world leaders provoke wars because they are thought to unite the electorate and make loyalty to the government a patriotic duty? Or is it that societies feel, like the doctors who applied the leeches to Lord Byron's temples, that an occasional bloodletting is essential to our health?

Whatever the reason, it seemed a good idea to sit in a garden where the roses bloom in winter and enjoy the moment of safety in a peaceful Arab country. All this was before the war which would end quite suddenly, when Saddam Hussein took my father's advice and avoided the temptation of doing anything heroic.

No weapons of mass destruction would be found and the Al Qaeda terrorists would turn up, alive and unharmed, in Saudi Arabia. The blasted ruins of Mesopotamia are to be repaired by companies close to President Bush's government, and the discovery of mass graves has persuaded us, if we need persuading, of the horrors of Saddam's regime. The Shias, the Sunnis and the Kurds are now free to quarrel with each other, and there is nothing, unhappily, to suggest that the times are likely to become less interesting.

16

Timing and the Art of Advocacy

The art of advocacy is not used only in courtrooms. Lovers pursuing their claims, parents persuading their children, businessmen after a bargain, salesmen trying to sell double glazing, husbands making excuses for absences and neglect, all have to find persuasive arguments, presenting their cases with as much charm as possible and hoping for a verdict of 'not guilty'. Pleas in mitigation have to be made to aggrieved partners. Arguments have to be won by searching questions. In all these situations tact is necessary and appropriate timing is essential.

My father once appeared in court for a comedian who told him, after the case had been won, that he greatly admired his timing. Rightly realizing that pauses, moments of, if possible, pregnant silence that keep the audience waiting eagerly were extremely effective, he adopted the practice of silently counting up to ten before he asked the first question in cross-examination. When I tried this, totally lacking his authority, the judge told me, quite crossly, to get 'on with it', and added, 'We can't all sit here watching you standing in silent prayer, you know.'

I admired another smoothly accomplished advocate, Cyril Salmon, who used to stroll negligently up and down the front bench, toying with a gold watch chain or cigar cutter, as he lobbed questions deftly over his shoulder at the witness box. When I tried this, another judge said, 'Do keep still! It's like watching ping-pong.'

Taking time requires a certain amount of courage. The vital words in the theatre and the law courts are 'slow down'. The most accomplished timer of jokes I ever encountered is the actor Leslie Phillips. Born into a poor family with a father who died young, he started his stage career at the age of eleven and has hardly been out of work since. He grew from a child actor into a juvenile lead in the 'Doctor' films and radio comedy. His way of saying 'Hellow!' in a drawn-out and lecherous manner made him famous. I met him first when he fell in love with my stepdaughter and there was a serious danger that he might end up calling me 'Dad' or, worse still, 'the Guvnor'. No marriage, however, took place. Leslie went on to play Falstaff and Gayev in *The Cherry Orchard* and, to my great delight, consented to be in a play of mine. His slow, amused, sardonic delivery delighted the audience but what I found most remarkable was his ability to get two laughs out of one joke.

The Leslie Phillips technique is to receive the feed line in silence but to act the response so that the audience is almost sure of what the answer's going to be. They feel safe to laugh for the first time. After a suitable wait, Phillips delivers the punch line and the audience laughs louder and again, because their guess has proved correct. Unhappily I had by this time left the bar and couldn't give his technique a try-out in court.

I'm also grateful to Leslie for a story he told me about a time when he was a young assistant stage manager in a West End theatre. The star was a well-known actor, famous for his infallible comic timing. At one point in the play he had to leave the stage with the leading lady and return immediately to answer the telephone. Accordingly they both left, but the male star didn't return. The audience was left to

149

enjoy the spectacle of an empty stage and listen to an unanswered telephone. When the actor's absence was further prolonged the young Leslie Phillips was sent to find him. He discovered him without difficulty making passionate love to the leading lady up against the ropes at the back of the stage. A tug on the back of the star's jacket merely got a command of, 'Go away, boy.' The audience had to endure another ten minutes of watching an empty stage. This is an example of very poor timing indeed.

Nothing delights an audience more than to have their suspicion of a joke, or the mystery which conceals a crime, confirmed. Much has been written about similarities between the law courts and the theatre — usually missing the point. However, talking to a jury has this in common with writing a story or unfolding the plot of a play. The first rule is not to be boring. This is hard in long cases about such matters as the evasion of value added tax and I remember, at the end of one such trial, congratulating the jury on having sat through what was undoubtedly one of the most tedious cases ever heard at the Old Bailey. The judge countered this by starting his summing-up, 'It may surprise you to know, members of the jury, that it is not the sole purpose of the criminal law of England to entertain Mr Mortimer.'

The rebuke was no doubt well phrased and entirely just. But awakening the imagination of a jury, making your listeners see themselves in strange circumstances, understanding the motives of a different, no doubt alien cast of characters — all this is necessary if a jury, or even a judge, is to arrive at the truth. Criminal responsibilities can't be judged by statistics, or social surveys, or even by referring to similar cases. It's necessary to imagine just what it would be like to be the man in the pub quarrel, the wife in the violent domestic dispute, the abused Asian student on the night in question in Kensington, Bradford or Birmingham Perry Bar.

Overacting in the theatre and law courts is finished. Gone and forgotten are the arrivals in court of such advocates as Sir Edward Marshall Hall. He was always preceded by a clerk carrying a pile of clean handkerchiefs, a second followed with a carafe of water and the third brought the air cushion. If the prosecution evidence got nasty, Marshall Hall would blow his nose, a sad and terrible trumpet, on each of the handkerchiefs. If it got worse, he would knock over the carafe of water. If it became really dangerous, he would slowly and deliberately blow up the air cushion until the jury could pay attention to nothing else.

John Maude, son of the actor Cyril Maude, who became an Old Bailey judge, used to announce that his client was going to give evidence in a criminal trial (always a dangerous proceeding) by saying, 'You can imagine what a nerve-racking experience it must be for anyone to go into that witness box, members of the jury. It must be terrible for the *innocent*. I will now call William Sykes' (or whatever his client's name might have been). So he conferred an aura of innocence on however shifty a character he was defending.

As in the world outside the courtroom, you can soon tell your friends from your enemies. The jury members who laugh at your jokes and those who greet them with expressions of stern disapproval, those who lean forward to be sure of catching every word of your cross-examination and those who put down their pencils and stare vaguely up to the ceiling. You have to decide between strengthening the resolve of your friends and trying to convert your enemies. By the time it comes to your final speech you'll hope to have done as much as possible of both. At the conclusion of the speech we all have our favourite peroration.

Marshall Hall had his great 'scales of justice' act. 'If you are in doubt, members of the jury,' he used to say, 'if you find the case for the defence and the prosecution evenly balanced' — here he would stretch his arms out like a pair of scales — 'then you must put into the defence side that little featherweight — the presumption of innocence.' And now one outstretched arm would sink. 'And the answer should be, must be, a verdict of not guilty!' One cynical judge told the jury he was always thankful when Sir Edward started his 'scales of justice' act because it meant that his speech would soon be coming to an end.

I worked out a slightly different conclusion. 'Members of the jury,' I used to say, 'tomorrow you will go back to your jobs and your homes. You will forget all about the Black Spot pub, the missing diary pages, the broken salad knife and the uneaten dog food at Number 12A Mafeking Avenue' (or whatever the particular facts of the case might have been). 'To you this has been only a short interruption. A minute part of your life. But to the man/

woman sitting there in the dock, it means the whole of his/her life. And we leave that life, with confidence, in your hands.' I thought this good enough to give to Rumpole, my fictional barrister, who was successful with it in a number of cases.

Things don't always run smoothly, however. A friend of mine had just embarked on the peroration of his final speech for the defence to an attentive jury when he saw that the judge was busily engaged in writing a note. When it was finished, it was folded and given to the usher, who brought it to my learned friend just as he had reached the most moving and dramatic moment. He paused and looked down at the note, which said, 'Dear Jim. I thought you'd like to know that your flies are open and I can see your cock.'

An advocate's life is not an easy one, and dangers and pitfalls should always be expected.

17

Male Clothing

Montaigne found it incredible that

> men alone should have been brought
> forth in a difficult and necessitous state
> which can only be sustained by bor-
> rowing from other creatures . . . if we
> had been endowed at birth with under
> garments and trousers there can be no
> doubt that Nature would have groomed
> those parts of us which remained ex-
> posed to the violence of the seasons
> with a thicker skin, as she has done for
> our finger tips and the soles of our feet.

As the process of evolution hasn't led to
our being born with trousers, men have to
choose an appearance in which to dress
themselves for life as an actor chooses
clothes for a part. It's a good and perhaps
the easiest thing to stick to the clothing of
the best part of your life, probably the

fashions of your youth.

My father wore spats to his work in the Probate, Divorce and Admiralty Division. Spats have now gone totally out of existence and the word is now used only for an argument or the past ejection of saliva. My father's spats were made of cloth that fastened under his feet and crossed his ankles and the top half of his shiny black boots. In summer his linen spats were white and he also wore a white waistcoat. In winter the waistcoat was black and the spats dark grey. He also wore a stiff winged collar with a bow tie, as Winston Churchill did, a gold watch chain across his stomach, a black jacket and dark striped trousers. He was uncomfortably aware of the words of one of the judges of the Probate, Divorce and Admiralty Division who had said to a less carefully dressed barrister, 'It gives me little pleasure to listen to a legal argument from a member of the bar wearing light grey trousers.'

When I was very young I collected cigarette cards portraying the great dandies. My favourite was Beau Brummell, who would cheerfully spend two hours attempting to tie the perfect cravat and who asked a fellow snappy dresser, out walking with the Prince Regent, 'Who's your fat friend?' I wrote up for a small walking stick (then known as a 'whangee') and a monocle, as I hoped to look like Bertie Wooster, a member of the Drones Club and the employer of the incomparable Jeeves, who enforced strict codes of clothing on his master.

I also wore a dinner jacket with a soft turned-down collar to my shirt (instead of the conventional stiff and upstanding variety). In this I was imitating King Edward VIII, who had fallen in love with an American divorcée and was about to abdicate. My father and I always wore dinner jackets when dining in hotels and restaurants or going to the theatre. When we turned up in evening dress at a cinema in Torquay the whole audience burst into spontaneous applause. At Harrow we wore top hats and tails on Sundays and for attending the annual cricket match against Eton. On this occasion a silver-topped cane with a dark blue tassel was also carried. The whole outfit caused considerable mirth on the Underground when you travelled on your way to Lord's.

At university I took, for a while, to purple corduroy trousers, bow ties and a large-brimmed sombrero. I would wear this outfit whilst smoking black Balkan

Sobranie cigarettes. I must have looked ridiculous. Luckily I started to go to the tailor in Oxford who has made my clothes ever since and who has a long record of my unfortunately expanding body. In this shop men are judged by their clothes. When a Mr Varney was in charge he said he couldn't bear to see Robin Day, a famous political commentator and interviewer on television. 'That Mr Day,' he said, 'is a national disgrace, an object of scorn and derision who should never be allowed to appear on television as the mere sight of him must cause universal pain and distress.' When I asked him what exactly was so appalling about Robin Day, he spoke as though naming the most unforgivable sin. 'I don't know who cuts his jackets,' he said, 'but when that Mr Day points his sleeve almost rides up to his elbow.'

I grew up in the days of 'sports jackets' made of tweed and preferably so well worn that they had leather round the cuffs and leather patches on the elbows. They were worn with cavalry-twill trousers and chukka boots to visit the saloon bar before Sunday lunch. Those were the days of three-piece suits and trousers with braces, although sock suspenders were already on the way out. A friend of mine laughed so loudly at Frank Sinatra's sock suspenders (she called them braces on his socks) when he prepared himself for an act of love that the great singer was deeply hurt and sex was taken off the menu. I survived, at least young at heart, into the era of Afghan waistcoats, velvet trousers, bangles, beads and Nehru jackets.

Since then I have reverted to the sort of clothing I wore when I emerged into life, became a barrister, published a first novel and took on a wife with four children and, in the years immediately following, would have two more. Costume designers, in period plays and films, seldom realize that men hope to preserve the appearance of their youth and may be as much as forty years behind the fashion. In *A Christmas Carol*, written in 1843, old Mr Fezziwig is still wearing a Welsh wig. So the fashions of today, unstructured suits, fleeces and baseball caps worn back to front, may still be decking out very old men in the year 2050.

Defence barristers down at the Old Bailey had to avoid looking too rich or too inexperienced. Gowns should be elderly, perhaps torn and inexpertly mended. Waistcoats were probably egg-stained. The wigs, obstinately retained since they were

159

the height of fashion, should be yellowing with age and, if possible, disintegrating. If one had to be bought new, an alarmingly expensive purchase, it should be kicked round the room and left out in the rain, a white wig being a sure sign of a far too recent call to the bar. This is Rumpole's courtroom appearance and was mine also. To it I added large cuff links which twinkled at the jury and, I hoped, retained their interest when all else failed.

Writers have been less anxious to conceal signs of success. Dickens appeared all decked out in gorgeous waistcoats with gold chains and rings, as did Disraeli. Oscar Wilde progressed from velvet knee breeches and carnations dyed green to curly brimmed bowler hats and coats with astrakhan collars. Nowadays any collection of writers is deliberately 'dressed down' like workers in city offices, determined to bond with each other by wearing only casual clothes on Fridays.

Finally, a few words of warning. T-shirts are unflattering to aged and scrawny necks, shoulder-length hair seems unsuitable when it's grey and ponytails trapped in an elastic band are always a danger. An exception to this rule is the shortish, neat, impeccably clean, grey to white ponytail of my friend Jon Lord, late of Deep Purple, now the composer of classical music. He also wears his ponytail with impressively dark clothing. Someone described Baudelaire's 'fine sombre clothing' and that always seemed to me a desirable way to dress. But then Baudelaire's hair was cropped very short, like, as they also said, *'une vraie toilette de la guillotine'*, so perhaps that's not such a good idea either.

18

Being Vulgar

Speaking of Byron, George Eliot called him 'the most vulgar-minded genius that ever produced a great effect on literature'. It's questionable if Byron's mind was notably vulgar. His sense of irony never deserted him, and when at his most tender, even sentimental, moments he couldn't resist laughing at himself:

> And Julia sate with Juan,
>   half embraced
> And half retiring from the glowing arm,
> Which trembled like the bosom where
>   'twas placed
> Yet still she must have thought there
>   was no harm,
> Or else 'twere easy to withdraw
>   her waist;
> But then the situation had its charm,
> And then — God knows what next —
>   I can't go on;
> I'm almost sorry that I e'er begun.

However, to deny all vulgarity to Byron would be grossly unfair. Vulgarity is not, as George Eliot would have it, something to be avoided at all costs. And you should not, in life or in literature, be afraid of sentimentality either. Some of the best things in life, works that are a pleasure to be handed on to the generations to come, have vulgarity and sentimentality in spades. And I don't mean seaside postcards or old music hall songs, but the greatest works of Dickens, Chaucer, Sterne, James Joyce and Rabelais. Indeed it's impossible to read through, say, the novels of Virginia Woolf without longing for a touch, a mere hint of vulgarity or sentimentality, a tear-jerking scene perhaps, or even a joke about a fart. Benjamin Britten and his circle of friends used to say that Puccini's operas 'are all right, it's just the music that's so terrible'. And yet you can be tearful at the end of *La Bohème* or be swept away by the shameless melodrama of *Tosca* more easily than by Britten's cold and more tasteful music.

And if Byron was vulgar-minded, how about Shakespeare? In the purely literary sense it's hard to criticize his poetry and infallible sense of drama. There are only very occasional over-ornate moments of showing off and sentimentality, as in:

> *And pity, like a naked new-born babe,*
> *Striding the blast, or heaven's*
>   *cherubim hors'd*
> *Upon the sightless couriers of the air,*
> *Shall blow the horrid deed in*
>   *every eye,*
> *That tears shall drown the wind . . .*

The more showy paintings of Rubens, the falling clouds of female flesh, might be described as vulgar, as might Toulouse-Lautrec's lesbians and prostitutes or the satirical drawings of George Grosz. Picasso could be vulgar but not, strangely enough, Matisse; and there is a tender vulgarity in Kurt Weill. Critics might say that the poetry of Rudyard Kipling, with its easy rhythms and populist appeal, is vulgar but this was the source of his confident mastery of verse. Vulgarity is, at least, energetic.

The actor Donald Wolfit, playing Shylock, sharpened his knife during the trial scene and then dropped it point downwards until it stood quivering, stabbing the stage. 'Terribly vulgar effect,' said Gielgud with a sniff of disapproval. And yet great acting, as practised by Laurence Olivier, had its elements of vulgar showing-off. He entered as Othello, blacked up and with a rose in his mouth. He died hanging upside down, his ankles grasped by terrified spear-carriers, as Coriolanus. He swooped down from a high ramp as Hamlet, holding the sword that killed Claudius like an avenging angel. He imagined the scream of pain a small animal might emit if it found its tongue frozen to the ice and gave it to the blinded Oedipus. He slid down the length of a stage curtain as Mr Puff in *The Critic.* Terribly vulgar indeed, but all wonderful moments in the theatre.

The Russian writer Nabokov thought Dostoyevsky vulgar and said that reading his books was like enjoying the more lurid crime stories in some sensational newspaper, which is perhaps why *Crime and Punishment* and *The Brothers Karamazov* exercise their compulsive fascination.

Oscar Wilde mocked Dickens for his vulgar sentimentality in writing the death of Little Nell. Perhaps Dickens didn't feel as strongly about Nell, for all her slightly embarrassing sweetness, as he did for Jo, the little crossing sweeper in *Bleak House.* And when Jo died of poverty and neglect he comes straight out of the book and steps down to the footlights:

Dead, your Majesty. Dead, my lords and gentlemen. Dead, Right Reverends and Wrong Reverends of every order. Dead, men and women, born with Heavenly compassion in your hearts. And dying thus around us every day.

You could say this is sentimental, which it is. You might find the effect vulgar. I know it to be magnificent.

In another sense Shakespeare has a healthy sense of vulgarity. Even his most serious texts are dotted with sexual innuendoes, and he didn't rule out fart jokes. Launce in *Two Gentlemen of Verona* takes personal responsibility for the indiscretion of his dog, Crab: 'he had not been there — bless the mark! — a pissing while, but all the chamber smelt him'. Shakespeare was also certain of a laugh from the groundlings when Pompey, in *Measure for Measure*, announces that his surname is Bum. 'Troth, and your bum is the greatest thing about you,' says Escalus, 'so that in the beastliest sense you are Pompey the Great.'

'Vulgar' was a term of abuse much used in my youth. It could be applied to furniture ('what a vulgar little chair'), seaside resorts (Brighton and Blackpool) and even after-dinner drinks (crème de menthe frappé). It was vulgar to say 'serviettes' instead of 'table napkins' or 'lounge' instead of 'sitting room'. Wearing a ready-made bow tie, or eating asparagus with a fork or peas on a knife, all such things were thought of as unforgivably vulgar. It was horribly vulgar to pour your tea into your saucer to cool it (once a common practice) or wear brown shoes with a blue suit or have a gnome in your front garden. There was a whole world of things which non-vulgar people, including, of course, the Bloomsbury group, would never permit. Harrow, among the English public schools, was thought of as 'vulgar', producing unreliable characters wearing scuffed suede shoes who drove battered sports cars and frequented gin palaces on the Great West Road. The alleged vulgarity of old Harrovians attracted John Betjeman so much that, although he had been to Marlborough, he used to put on a Harrovian boater and sit at the piano playing Harrow school songs. Nothing excited him more than carefully observed vulgarity.

Such definitions of vulgarity belong to an arcane snobbery and a vanished standard of good taste. Now political correctness has tried to enforce an artificial code of polite conduct on our basic instinct to laugh at most things, including, sex, death and going to the lavatory. In life and in literature there may still be opportunities to show off, exaggerate, embellish and startle. The only advice I would give to those who come after me is, 'If you can find a streak of vulgarity in yourself, nurture it.'

19

The Marketplace

My uncle Harold was rich. I think that in the 1930s, when such things were more rare, he was a millionaire. His father had owned a furniture shop in Tottenham Court Road and a patented bed spring. He left the shop to his other son, Ambrose Heal, and the bed spring to my uncle Harold. Out of this device, by the time he married my aunt Marjorie, Harold owned a factory at Staples Corner, on the outskirts of London, making mattresses which were so comfortable that King George V, having hurt his back during the 1914–18 war, chose to sleep on one.

My rich uncle was mildly eccentric. He had his waistcoats made with flannel flaps behind to keep his bottom warm. He designed his own wide-brimmed hats and drove a Lagonda. He was also superstitious, refusing to walk under ladders or have lilies in the house, and feared the thirteenth of each month. In the taste of the 1930s he designed some good furniture, including the desk I am writing on now. Towards the end of his life, he flew into a terrible temper with my aunt because she wrote a shopping list out on a clean envelope. In spite of his wealth, he considered this a terrible waste.

I don't think we ever envied my uncle's wealth, the Lagonda and the country estate with the cottages in which the workers would be given boxes of biscuits and pounds of tea at Christmas. All this took place in the days when doctors, lawyers, schoolteachers, even architects were thought to follow useful, valuable callings, with rules against professional misconduct. Millionaires seemed to us, on the whole, to be something of a joke.

We scarcely ever heard the word 'entrepreneur' and if we did it was used to describe the middleman who produced nothing. He intervened between the manufacturer and the consumer and made easy money out of both of them. Now entrepreneurs are thought to follow the most worthwhile of all professions and every child, in the market-oriented way of New Labour education, should be taught the art of becoming one. Indeed, this calling has been judged to rank so high in the field of human endeavour that President Bush, in one of his wilder flights of verbal confusion, was heard to say, 'The trouble with the French is that they haven't got a word for "entrepreneur".'

The change became complete in the Thatcher years. As the factory gates closed there were no jobs for manufacturers any more and we became a nation of shop-keepers and hairdressers. It was then that politicians, 'entrepreneurs' and practically everyone else began to speak, in tones of religious awe, about the 'marketplace'. Ignore the fact that Jesus made some un-called-for remarks about the poor being blessed, forget the sometimes uncommercial nature of art or literature that reveals the truth about our lives, and instead take everything down to the marketplace to discover how it sells and how much it's worth.

All this comes as something of a surprise to those of us who know marketplaces. From Portobello and the Caledonian Road to the great souk of Marrakech, they are places for the quick disposal of stolen property, where you will be offered sham antiques and quack medicines, where you can have your wallet and your bottom pinched, where you may be sold a dead bat as a sovereign cure for sciatica, or tickets for a non-existent lottery, and where some seemingly helpful and committed guide will lead you, infallibly, to the shop owned by his relatives in order that you may be deceived over the price of carpets. And if it's said that the great, established businesses or the world's global corporations have little in common with the back streets of Marrakech, you have only to remember Enron and its accountants and directors to appreciate that marketplaces are where no sucker ever gets an even break.

The other mantra of the Thatcher era was 'consumer choice' and this conception lingers on as the great opportunity of our times. The heavenly marketplace, if it is to do its job properly, must be furnished with at least fifty-seven varieties of everything. Anyone who has fewer than this number of varieties of yoghurt to choose from is not living life to the full. And to see this blessing working at its best you must 'shop around', which means, I suppose, trudging wearily from one supermarket to another, comparing the price of cornflakes.

The idea that a wide choice is always a desirable, or even a useful, part of life can be tested in the cases of restaurants and television. You know that when you are handed a heavy menu, bound in vellum with a dangling gold tassel, offering you fifteen choices of everything, you can be sure none of it will be any good. Eat somewhere where the whole offering is chalked up on a short board and it's likely to be profoundly satisfactory.

In the best period of television there were only two choices, so that a play or a film commanded a huge and united audience. As the choices multiplied the programmes, reduced to a desperate grab for ratings, noticeably deteriorated. But the remorseless process goes on until the viewer can enjoy the luxury of flicking through fifty channels of identical rubbish. With not enough money, or advertising, to provide for all these outlets, what the audience is offered is what Proverbs called 'a small choice of rotten apples'.

The doctor who makes a friend of his patients, the lawyer who defends death penalty cases in distant countries for no fee, the schoolteacher who opens a child's eyes to a new world of books and poetry — such people do nothing that can be measured in marketplaces. The greatest painters, composers and writers don't offer you choices, they present you with what only they can do, and you must take it or leave it. So when such subjects as the values of the marketplace are discussed, you will probably not have much to contribute. You can repeat a poem in your head and wait until the conversation is over. But if anyone starts talking about 'level playing fields', get up and steal quietly from the room.

20

Law or Justice

As I have said, my first encounter with the law was in the Probate, Divorce and Admiralty Division. Probate cases were the ones in which ruthless relatives fought tooth and nail for the furniture. Admiralty cases, where the judge sat in front of a large anchor and seafaring men arrived unrolling charts, were closed books to us and called for specialist lawyers with a knowledge of salvage and chartering vessels. Divorce was sexier, more dramatic and supplied our daily bread, so that in my childhood I was housed, fed, watered, clothed and educated almost entirely on the proceeds of adultery, cruelty and wilful neglect to provide reasonable maintenance.

The divorce laws at the time I started life as a barrister, in the late 1940s, dramatically illustrated the gulf between the law and reality, the law and morality or, in many cases, the law and justice.

Today, of course, ending a marriage is a matter of filling out a form, dividing up the property and saying, 'Cheerio!' When I started practice you had to prove something extremely serious like cruelty or adultery. One of my first clients was a husband, longing to end his marriage, who was finding it extremely hard to discover anyone prepared to commit adultery with his wife. He was reduced to the horrifying expedient of disguising himself in a false beard, a false moustache and a pair of dark glasses and creeping into his own bungalow, in full view of the neighbours, pretending to be his own co-respondent. The plot was discovered and the unfortunate husband was sent to prison for 'perverting the course of justice'. I thought this was extremely hard. If you can't sleep with your own wife wearing a false beard, what can you do? His case showed, however, in an extreme form, an unbridgeable gap between the law, justice, morality or even common sense.

Matrimonial law had come down from the ecclesiastical courts, through the years when women couldn't own property or divorce their husbands for adultery, unless it was coupled with cruelty. It had been humanized to some extent by the writer and independent MP A.P. Herbert in the 1930s, but when I started just after the war a husband could still get damages from his wife's lover. This entailed an argument in court about her value in hard cash. In these unseemly proceedings, a husband had to argue that his wife was a fabulous cook, mother and lover and therefore worth a great deal. The ungallant lover, however, swore she was a cold fish in bed and never did the washing-up. There was no such thing as a divorce by consent; in fact consent was called 'connivance' and was a bar to freedom from an unhappy marriage.

In these circumstances lawyers, and very often judges, had to achieve fair and reasonable solutions for their unhappy clients, not only with no assistance from the law but very often in spite of it. This raises the question, do laws have to be respected and obeyed simply because they're there?

Once again it's a poet's imaginings which provide the most helpful debate and throw the brightest light on this question. *Measure for Measure* tells of an old, rarely used Viennese law making fornication punishable by death. The Duke, like God taking a sabbatical, leaves the city and appoints as his regent the puritanical, rigorous, painfully virtuous Angelo. The normal and perfectly harmless young Claudio is guilty of what the brothel keeper's servant, Pompey, calls 'Groping for trouts in a peculiar river'. Mistress Overdone, with a duller use of language, says Claudio is to have 'his head . . . chopped off . . . for getting Madam Julietta with child'. Angelo is dedicated to the belief that the letter of the law has to be obeyed and to hell with natural justice.

The debate starts when Escalus, 'an ancient Lord' and servant of the Duke who, full of humanity and common sense, is another of Shakespeare's favourite characters, tries to plead Claudio's case, asking Angelo to think:

Whether you had not sometime in your life
Err'd in this point which now you censure him,
And pull'd the law upon you.

Angelo's answer is simple. 'We must not make a scarecrow of the law' so it becomes a 'perch' and not a 'terror' for ravens and lawless birds. Furthermore, our own possible weaknesses are no excuse for not strictly enforcing the legal code. ' 'Tis one thing to be tempted, Escalus,' he says. 'Another thing to fall.' A jury condemning a thief to death, he agrees, may contain a 'thief or two / Guiltier than him they try,' but that makes no difference to the laws we all have to obey. Don't tell me about my guilty thoughts, Angelo is saying, but 'When I, that censure him, do so offend / Let mine own judgement pattern out my death'.

The theoretical debates become drama when Claudio's beautiful sister, Isabella, on the point of becoming a nun, comes to plead for her brother's life. Angelo lusts after her and feels himself sorely tempted to go groping for trouts just like the criminal he despises. Before the breakdown of Angelo the seagreen incorruptible, in his scenes with Isabella, the conflict between the strict upholder of the letter of the law and natural justice is played out.

At first Angelo is obdurate: 'Your brother is a forfeit of the law, / And you but waste your words.' 'Why, all the souls that were were forfeit once,' Isabella reminds him. 'And He that might the vantage best have took / Found out the remedy.' So there is a power greater than the law, that of Christ who redeemed all our sins, who broke the strict laws of the

Pharisees and died a convicted criminal. 'How would you be,' she asks Angelo, 'if He, which is the top of judgement, should / But judge you as you are?' This is Escalus's argument returning. What we regard as the just process of criminal trials is not much more than sinful human beings punishing each other. True religion points the way to a more merciful process.

But not always. The law is never more cruel, or more oblivious to the arguments of Escalus and Isabella, than when it claims to have God on its side. The proceedings of the Inquisition and the Shia laws, if enforced in Islamic states, can outdo the ancient criminal code of Vienna in wanton ferocity. A modern Angelo might be a regent in the Middle East prepared to order an errant wife to be stoned to death. And, in Europe, who would Isabella have to call on in this faithless age? No God, perhaps; but is there, in the bravest hearts, some system of natural justice better than current laws can provide? Can there be?

The answer must depend on the view you take of the human condition. Are people naturally destructive, immoral, predatory and self-seeking, only to be kept in order by harsh laws and fiercely deterrent mandatory sentences? Or are men and women naturally orderly, merciful, humane and bred with a need for justice and mutual aid? Of course these qualities, or defects, are not evenly distributed, and undoubtedly there is much of each in all of us, but when it comes to the law some sort of distinction can be drawn. Are you a Shylock or a Bassanio?

Shylock pinned his faith on the words in the contract, the nature of his bond and the duty of the state to uphold the letter of the law regardless of human suffering. Bassanio put another point of view. More important than the sanctity of the law was the plight of the individual parties in the particular case. If the enforcement of contracts were all-important, a man would die with a pound of flesh carved off near to his heart. Therefore Bassanio pleads to Portia, who has come to judge the case: 'And I beseech you / Wrest once the law to your authority: / To do a great right, do a little wrong, / And curb this cruel devil of his will.' So forget the wording of the statute, ignore the terms of the contract, and, in the name of natural justice, do what you think is right.

The late Lord Denning, a man full of charm who passed judgement in short, workman-like sentences spoken in a carefully preserved Hampshire accent, always said he was a 'Bassanio man'. What was important to him was justice in the individual case and not the omnipotence of the law. His decisions, on this basis, led to frequent appeals to the House of Lords, where the judges, apparently more sympathetic to Shylock's line of legal argument, frequently reversed his decisions. The gulf will still exist and Isabellas will be appealing to Angelos to show a little humanity far into the future.

Perhaps she could have a word with the judges in the new, politically correct divorce courts, which have swung round to a different absurdity. In one of the last cases I was concerned with, a husband returning unexpectedly one afternoon to his home in Golders Green found his wife enjoying sex with three members of a pop group. To pay for her entertainment he found, after the divorce, that he had to sell his house and his business to give her half of all he possessed as well as half of his future earnings. I hasten to say that the law is not sexist in this respect. A famously successful woman writer, finding her husband in bed with her secretary, had to reward him equally and was faced with a similar financial disaster.

A judge who also had medical qualifications once told me the following story. He was trying, long ago, a perfectly friendly action between a woman's husband and her lover to determine which of them, and they were both well off, should pay for her child's education and future support. The parties agreed to a blood test and when the judge got the report it was perfectly clear that neither of the two men before him, but some third, possibly penniless, stranger must be the father of the child. He tore up the report, threw it into the wastepaper basket and invited the two men to his room. There he told them that the blood test had established nothing with any clarity and that they should agree to share the cost of bringing up the child. What he did was certainly against the law and, just as certainly, right.

21

Family Values

When you hear a politician lecturing the nation on the subject of family values you know that he (it's almost always a he) has probably left a weeping wife at home, has quarrelled with his children and is having it off with his 'work experience' researcher. No doubt there are many happy families, and they're not all the same, but close families, like the quiet country cottages Sherlock Holmes observed from the train, can be torture chambers for those imprisoned in them. Murder has this in common with Christmas, most of it goes on in the family circle.

Family values, down the centuries, have not had a particularly good press in literature — unless you count the works of Dickens, who, in real life, nailed up the door which led to his wife's bedroom. The domestic murder in a bath and the subsequent curse upon the house of Atreus, the

184

unhappy state of the Danish royal family when a prince's father was poisoned by his uncle, the ghastly dinner parties hosted by the Macbeths when ghosts were on the guest list don't make encouraging reading for newlyweds. The home lives of Henry VIII, the Crippens or Mary Queen of Scots don't encourage family values.

Violence, betrayal, lingering curses and sudden death aren't the only drawbacks to family life. Even as politicians are parading its virtues you can hear across the country the sound of stifled yawns. Mrs Patrick Campbell, in some ways an unlikely propagandist for marriage, spoke of it as 'the deep, deep peace of the double bed after the hurly-burly of the chaise-longue'. The trouble with double beds is that people tend to go to sleep in them. When I did divorce cases I found that couples, married to other partners, had enthusiastic and apparently deeply satisfactory love affairs until a divorce set them free to marry. When they did so the excitement evaporated. There were no more furtive telephone calls, no element of danger when they listened for a creaking stair or an unexpected key in the front door, no hours snatched in the back of a Ford Cortina parked in a dark wood. It all became legal, respectable and above board and, in many sad cases, they went off it.

Even the most happily married have a certain admiration for illicit lovers, who were always the heroes and heroines of ancient literature. Lancelot is a more attractive figure than King Arthur, Cleopatra than Octavia. We were once delayed for three hours at Heathrow Airport while an aged engineer with a beard did something to the pipes. The captain, a handsome middle-aged man with greying sideboards, carried his cap under his arm and walked among us from time to time, sympathizing with our frustration and promising that all would be well. When we finally rose into the air his gently reassuring voice came over the Tannoy. 'This is your captain, Johnny Montague-Smith. We are now on our way and I can assure you that this aircraft is completely safe. If it weren't I wouldn't be in it because I have no intention at all of dying in a plane crash. My dear old father told me that the only decent way for an English gentleman to die is shot through the heart in the bed of his best friend's wife.'

From there on we all, even the most respectably married, had every faith in Captain Johnny Montague-Smith and believed

him when he said he wouldn't die in an
aeroplane crash.

With out chained friend,
perhaps a jealous foe,
The dreariest and the longest
journey go.

So wrote Shelley, whom Byron found the
'least selfish' and 'mildest of men', de-
nouncing marriage as though he were a fu-
gitive from a chain gang. Such dire warnings as this, and the American who said
that marriage is very like a Florida hurri-
cane, 'it starts off with all that sucking and
blowing and you end up by losing your
house', do more for family life than the
hard sell of unreliable politicians. Because
it's not as grim as all that. You may well
find a true friend and not a deadly foe and
the journey shouldn't be entirely dreary.
Children who like their parents to be married are our only tenuous claim to immortality.

In the future, when it's taken over by my
heirs, there may be changes in the business
of childbirth, when science becomes involved, with far-reaching results. Last week
we were in New York to see the opening of
a film starring my attractive actor son-in-

law Alessandro. He also has a handsome, charming brother. They are members of an Italian-American family and have the fine looks of their Sardinian artist grandfather, who arrived penniless in New York in 1942 and was lucky not to be met with our present 'crackdown' on asylum seekers. After the opening of a film he starred in, Alessandro had a meeting with one of the film's executives, who inquired if he'd mind asking his father to donate his sperm to her lesbian girlfriend. Surprisingly enough, Alessandro's father, an adviser to the government in Washington, was reluctant to do so.

Family life is going to take a battering from a new law suggested by politicians who proclaim its values; and this also concerns sperm donors. Those actors who have rested too long, or men of other professions down on their luck, who wank for a few pounds and provide a supply for would-be parents in difficulty must now make their names and identities known to the families they help to create. You can see horrendous scenes following. The resting actor might win the lottery and be sued for the maintenance of all the children his part-time occupation produced. Or, perhaps worse, the wanker for money might want to claim 'his' children and take over the family.

Worse still, parents are to be compelled to tell their children whom their natural, or sperm-giving, father was. As a considerable percentage of children born in marriage are not in fact fathered by their mother's husband, secrets will be suddenly revealed to everyone's embarrassment and a sudden rise in the divorce rate will follow. Jewish custom, which traces descent solely from the mother, is more sensible and more discreet. Our own lawgivers can't accept the fact that there are many things in family life that are best kept shrouded in mystery.

Family life, in my experience, far from being dull and secure, is a constantly unfolding drama. One Saturday evening, at our home in the country, my youngest daughter had brought home a boyfriend with whom her relationship was over. He was naturally depressed, possibly suicidal. Alessandro's mother was staying with us and preparations for his and my daughter Emily's wedding were gripping the household like the production of a major film. In the kitchen where we assembled, the cat, who lives a secret life in and out of the upstairs windows, entered in pursuit of a mouse. The cat was pursued by a liberated

Jack Russell, who showed every sign of wanting to eat it. With her nerves already at breaking point, my fox-hunting wife grabbed the mouse and prepared to kill it with a single blow from the wooden hammer more often used to flatten steaks. This led to a general uproar of protest from my daughters, the ex-boyfriend and Alessandro's mother. Raising the hammer, my wife was resolute. 'If this mouse lives,' she said, 'there'll be eight more mice in the world before you've had time to count.' As the argument increased there was a gentle knock on the kitchen door and Elizabeth, our neighbour from a mile down the hill, entered holding a cup. 'Can any of you spare a little of that liquid you use for cleaning contact lenses?' was what she asked.

In her surprise, my wife relaxed her grip on the mouse, which made a dash for freedom. The cat was gathered up, the Jack Russell expelled and the now ex-boyfriend cheered up. Family values were seen at their best.

22

Missed Opportunities

'I'm not very good at sex, Jane. But with you I'll really *try*,' is a pretty hopeless sort of approach to any woman, but I'm assured it was said to a friendly publicist by one of her more serious and not entirely successful authors. Equally hopeless are such gambits as 'My wife doesn't understand me,' or, even worse, 'Sex with you would do wonders for my prose style.' If you want to improve your prose style, read Gibbon, Lytton Strachey, Evelyn Waugh and Hemingway. If you want to make love it is better to say so plainly, without claiming any literary reward for your trouble.

My wife overheard a different, more sporting approach on the hunting field. A would-be lover rode up to a handsome, lively middle-aged woman and said, 'I say, Daphne, how about a gun in your shoot?' The reply was, I'm afraid, disappointing. 'No thanks,' she said, 'I'm fully syndicated at the moment.'

It's well known that John Betjeman, summing up his regrets on his deathbed, said, 'Not enough sex,' and it is the missed opportunities of your youth that will haunt your old age. I shall never forget the friendly girl who, long ago, said, 'Let's go down to Soho and do something sordid.' I, in my stupidity, thought she was suggesting some rather dirty restaurant and turned down the offer. There will be a long future of kicking yourself for not understanding such simple approaches as, 'Where will you be spending the night?' and you answered, 'I'd better be going home. I've got a lot to do in the morning.' A lot to do! Whatever it was has long been forgotten; what will always be remembered is the night that didn't happen.

It's often said that men desire women for their looks but women fancy men for some less reliable quality, like their characters or their supposed position in the world. We, the vast majority of non-beautiful people, can only hope this is true.

If it is, it puts men at an unfair advantage. If you work hard at it, you might be able to improve your character, or even your position in the world. Beauty is something you can do absolutely nothing about.

It is distributed in the most unfair, politically incorrect and anti-democratic manner. It is bestowed on the least deserving and often denied to the best, unselfish and kindly intentioned people. Quite often the unfair nature of this gift causes resentment, not only from jealous women. I have known beautiful girls who have been badly treated and slighted by men who feel eclipsed by such spanking looks.

I have a beautiful wife and beautiful daughters and I would never say they don't deserve such luck. The fact is mildly surprising, however, as I look, as some newspaper put it kindly, 'like a bag of spanners'. The great majority of male spanner look-alikes must work out a careful approach and avoid anything as hopeless as promising to try hard. Stendhal, no oil painting but a man who notched up his conquests on his braces, relied on laughter and boasted, perhaps truthfully, that he could beat the record of the best-looking men. There is much to be said for this approach. My experience as a counsel for the defence down at the Old Bailey was that if you could get the jury laughing you were likely to win the case. The more solemn the proceedings became, the less happy the verdict was likely to be.

If it's not true that men are loved only for their characters, or their positions of power, it's equally mistaken to believe that all women are called upon to be reproductions of Miss Dynamite or Catherine Zeta-Jones. One of the miracles of life is that few people pass through it without finding someone to love them. Awkward, even impossible people find love and it's a great convenience if they find it with each other. As someone said, it was very kind of God to arrange for Thomas Carlyle to marry Jane Carlyle, because 'it meant that only two people were unhappy instead of four'.

The mysterious forces which compel the most unlikely to dedicate their lives to each other can't be explained. I can only repeat that missed opportunities, in life and love, may haunt you for ever. Opportunities should be taken gratefully, even if the results may be somewhat bizarre. Long ago, in the distant days of Angus Steak Houses and Mateus Rosé and Frankie Vaughan singing 'Give Me the Moonlight', I took a new-found friend out to dinner. Later I drove her back to her flat in a London square in which the front doors were flanked by rows of bells for different apartments. She suggested I come up to hers after I'd parked the car. Before she left me she touched her hair and said, 'I'd better warn you. All this comes off.'

Left alone in the car, I came to the conclusion that what she had told me meant that she was bald. Did I want to get into bed with a bald-headed woman? No, I did not. Should I not then turn the car around and drive straight home without any further explanation? Perhaps. But wouldn't that be a cowardly, even a mean and unkind thing to do? It wasn't, after all, her fault that she was bald and it would be dreadful to remind her of the fact in such a dramatic fashion. I hit on another solution. I'd take my glasses off. My sight is so short that I wouldn't be able to see how bald she was.

After I'd parked the car I rang the top bell, as I had seen her do beside the front door, and was rewarded by a deeply sexy voice saying, 'Come upstairs.' I obeyed, with my glasses off, and found the top flat's door opened by a blurred but distinctly bald figure wearing a dressing gown. I threw my arms round it, only to discover it was a bald-headed, quite elderly man and I was in the wrong house.

Having beaten a hasty and apologetic retreat, I finally got to the right flat and found that my companion had perfectly acceptable hair which had been covered with a wig. It was, as I say, a bizarre evening but not one I've lived to regret.

23

Making a Fuss

At one time, again it was in the time of my
youth, the hotels, the restaurants, the
railway stations of England rang to the
sound of middle-aged, middle-class men
making a fuss. Cold plates, warm drinks,
late trains, slow waiters would set them off
in a roar. Their voices, raised in anger,
could be heard in Europe as they progressed from Calais to the Promenade des
Anglais in Cannes, complaining about the
state of the lavatories or the inadequacy of
the breakfasts.

They had, no doubt some of them had,
been unhinged by the 1914–18 war. We
had a prep school master who used to
shout, 'Strafe and shell you, boy!' as he
hurled books at our heads and then,
wretchedly apologetic, compensated us
with small gifts of money. Our young ears
were blasted by middle-aged rage. For the
children of such men, life was a perpetual

embarrassment; you had to pretend that the red-faced aggrieved adult seated at your table was no sort of relation.

The law courts, in these early days, echoed with ill-temper. There was a judge who used to throw his pencil down in a pet and call out in a loud voice, 'We are not a stable!' if he thought his court wasn't receiving the respect it deserved. Another would greet a nervous barrister by saying, 'If you want to practise I suggest you practise at home.' Offended advocates would bang out of courts; clerks would have to be sent to reconcile them to judges who had gone too far. Even without such interruptions, proceedings were often unfriendly. 'Your argument, Mr Smith,' said one judge to the future Lord Birkenhead, 'is simply going into one of my ears and out of the other.'

'Perhaps, my Lord,' was the advocate's reply, 'that's because there's nothing in between.'

When the judge, further goaded, said, 'Why do you think I'm sitting here, Mr Smith?' the answer was, 'It's not for me to inquire into the inscrutable ways of providence.'

Birkenhead was highly skilled at turning a fuss to his advantage. Having failed to be elected as a member of the Reform Club, he habitually, when passing its doors, called in to use its lavatory. After many anxious meetings, the committee decided it was time to make a fuss and a fuss, of a surprisingly gentle sort, was made by the secretary. He met the peer on his way out of the Gents. 'Lord Birkenhead,' he fussed politely, 'I've been asked to remind you that this *is* a members' club.'

'Oh, really?' His Lordship did his best to sound interested. 'Is it that *as well?*'

Unless you have Birkenhead's gift for repartee it's unwise to lose your temper in court. You may, of course, make a considerable fuss, and even pretend extreme anger, but to lose it in reality would be extremely dangerous. In real life the ability to make a fuss has been secretly curtailed by the intolerance of children. In my childhood we listened patiently when our fathers bellowed protests against waiters who invariably interrupted their best stories just before the punch line by asking, 'Who's having the fish?'

Now if you go into a shop and interrupt the conversation behind the counter by asking for a little help in choosing the lingerie, your children will flee from you, hide behind the coats, pretend you're not related or even set off for home. It's a battle you can't win, so it's better to keep quiet, or reserve your fussing for worthier issues, such as the destruction of the presumption of innocence or other matters in which the children may allow you to fuss.

Dickens — not, as I have said, perfect in his attention to family values — could make a magnificent and effective fuss when the occasion demanded it. He wrote *Nicholas Nickleby* and put an end to ghastly Yorkshire schools. He derided and scorned the law's unbearable delays, the Poor Law and the hopeless inefficiency of government bureaucracy. He discovered that there were more than 100,000 London children who had no education, even at a 'ragged school'. And the ragged schools he visited were very ragged indeed, filled with children living by thieving and prostitution, filthy, illiterate and 'with all the deadly sins let loose'. He was moved to give a lecture, or write a pamphlet, on the desperate plight of children who slept in doorways, under bridges and in saw-pits. Happily he didn't write a pamphlet but produced *A Christmas Carol*, in which what he called the 'doomed children' appear as Ignorance and Want, sheltering under the cloak of the Spirit of Christmas Present.

So fuss as much as you like about poverty, overcrowded prisons, locked-up children and social injustice, or even the abolition of outdoor sex, but lay off the waiter.

It's not that young people can't make fusses for themselves. In fact they have taken the place of the middle-aged, middle-class man in protesting at the unfairness of life, the disgusting ostentation of their parents' car or their mother's consumption of cigarettes. Sometimes their fusses can be well phrased and effective.

We were travelling to Australia for a family Christmas in the sun when Emily's then boyfriend, a talented actor, joined the plane at Singapore and, although booked in steerage, joined my daughter in club class, sharing her seat and starting to snog her enthusiastically. Sitting next to them, it was my turn to pretend that I was no relation, until the steward arrived and told the lover that he was embarrassing those seated in club class and would he kindly return to the tourists.

At this he stood up and, projecting in a way that might have been heard throughout the plane, declaimed, 'Very well. But, everyone, look at this! This is what they did to Romeo and Juliet.'

24

Giving Money to Beggars

You should, I think, provided you have any of it at all, give money to beggars.

Begging is, after all, an ancient and honourable profession. Indian priests depended entirely on the contents of their begging bowls, monks and wandering friars begged for Jesus. Giving money to beggars produces a minor sense of generosity and well-being in the giver and some immediate satisfaction in the recipient. Such pleasant transactions are anathemas to those New Puritans who now rule us, and may survive to rule over you, the heirs to this testament. As in the grim reign of Oliver Cromwell, begging is to be made a criminal offence (in the days of the Great Protector, actors were subject to the same law). So the street sleepers, the unhappy children who have left home after a domestic row, the confused ageing women sleeping under newspapers, all of whom put their hands out to you as you pass from the theatre to the restaurant, will be given criminal convictions and moved, at huge public expense, from the nests they have made in doorways and under arches to Her Majesty's Prisons.

I spent some time talking to the street sleepers in an area of London between Lincoln's Inn Fields and the Embankment. They included middle-aged men who couldn't cope with filling in forms, paying rent and taxes, applying for jobs they didn't get or queuing up for public assistance. There was also a man who had been the manager of a supermarket with a car, holidays on the Costa Brava and a wife he loved very much who left him to go off with a soldier. After a period of misery he met an Italian girl at evening classes. They got married but she and their baby were run down and killed on a pedestrian crossing. This was too much for him. He locked up his house, posted his key back through the letter box and went to live on the streets.

The dedicated street sleepers, the respectable beggars who are no longer young, don't want to move into hostels where they might be attacked by young tearaways and have the few possessions they wander around with all day stolen. They don't go entirely without food. Four-wheel drives from the Home Counties come, often accompanied by a vicar intent on good works, and soup is ladled out. Late at night they get the leftover sandwiches from Marks & Spencer in bin liners. By this time they have become quite choosy, throwing out the BLTs in a search for the prawn and mayo. Except on the coldest nights, street-sleeping suits them so well that an elderly lady who had been taken into hospital begged to be rescued by her friends. They called at the hospital and managed, looking, I suppose, like porters, to trundle her out of the building in her bed and push her down to her preferred sleeping place — under the arches of an office block not far from the river.

These arches provide the four-star accommodation. Underneath them it's dry and out of the wind, and the regulars have their places reserved with their trannies and paperbacks, their blankets and old newspapers, all ready for the night. Do they beg? Well, of course they do. If you can get a place at the end of Hungerford Bridge you can make thirty pounds on a good day. Not many of them get this prime spot. It may go to the younger generation, who sleep where the heat comes up from the kitchens behind the Strand Palace Hotel.

Are they aggressive? I have to say that I haven't met an aggressive beggar in London. In New York, crossing 58th Street from the Plaza Oyster Bar to the Wyndham Hotel, I came up against a huge black man in a long, dark overcoat who said, in deep and threatening tones, 'Give me fifty dollars!' I managed to ask him if he would be content with thirty-five and, rather to my surprise, he said, 'All right, give me thirty-five dollars!' And so the deal was done.

Before we dismiss all those asking for our loose change as criminals, we should consider whether we're not all beggars. Every morning a shoal of letters and faxes arrives at my home begging for money for dozens of different causes, from the provision of deaf aids in African villages to funding a Conceptual Arts Centre in East Anglia. Many of the requests are persuasive and the causes worthy and they come with shiny brochures, well-designed graphics and forms asking for sums of money beyond the wildest dreams of anyone sitting in front of a saucer on the end of Hungerford Bridge.

The great and the good give lunches, or evenings with champagne and canapés, on the terrace of the House of Lords, at which they can beg from each other and solicit money for each other's favourite charities. I have gone begging for the Royal Court Theatre, the Howard League for Penal Reform, various other theatres and institutions, with my hand shamelessly held out to tycoons, managers of trust funds and government representatives. Like the street sleepers on the Embankment, I have tried to shame total strangers into parting with their loose change.

We don't beg only for money. We beg for love, doing our best to look needy and anxious to please. The world of advertising is devoted to begging people to spend money on things they may not really need. Politicians, those who seek to imprison far more honest and straightforward beggars, beg shamelessly for votes in exchange for promises they are never going to keep.

So what should be done about beggars? The confused and, perhaps, abused young who have left home after a quarrel clearly need looking after. But the older practitioners who have mismanaged their lives, or even prefer the freedom of the streets, should be left to exercise a profession more honourable than that of many bankers, share pushers or sellers of pension schemes. They will need your help from time to time in their efforts, which should be warmly welcomed by the New Labour government, to transfer the business of welfare to the private sector.

25

Eating Out

I have already advised you to avoid restaurants which offer multiple choices, twelve starters, fifteen main courses, all sorts of puddings, described on shiny paper in a menu bound in scarlet with gold tassels. As with the choices offered nowadays on television, these are likely to provide no more than a wide selection of rubbish.

There are other basic rules, such as avoiding any restaurant where the name of the chef is known to the public; still worse if he — it always seems to be a 'he' — appears on television. Also run a mile from any eatery where the waiter starts to lecture you on the food. Conversation, in some highly expensive joints I have visited, has ground to a halt during the cheese course while Damon or Jasper, our waiter for the evening, gives a lengthy talk on the history of the Caerphilly, or describes the exact amount of fermentation undergone by the *chèvre* from the valley of the Loire. All you need to do while you're eating cheese is to get on with the argument, or the reconciliation, the friendship or the remotely possible consummation you came out for.

Worse even than lectures about the cheese are instructions on how to eat. I have been in a Florida restaurant where we were fitted up with bibs like so many middle-aged babies and talked down through the crab. The language was that used to land aeroplanes in distress and the same calm, reassuring voice was adopted by the waiter: 'Grasp the claw firmly in the left hand and crack the hard shell of the claw with the instrument provided. A sharp pressure should produce a crack which will enable you to scoop out the crab flesh. This you can dip into either the French mayonnaise or the Thousand Island Sauce.'

Food in France, Italy or China is based on peasant cooking and has been handed down from grandmothers to mothers and daughters, who stick to traditional dishes. Supermarkets, fast-food outlets and the American cultural invasion have diminished our home cooking and most of our restaurants have lost all contact with the food we used to think of as traditionally English. Boiled mutton and caper sauce, baked jam roll, even steak and kidney pudding seem as remote as bowler hats or cherrywood pipes. Dominating star chefs have broken with the past and we are no longer the land of roast duck and apple sauce, roast lamb and mint sauce (a delicacy which always puzzled the French), but the country of rocket and sun-dried tomatoes, monkfish artfully arranged with pink sauce, a single peeled prawn and a sprig of dill, or a little castle made of venison doused in redcurrant coulis, which has also been used to draw patterns on the side of the plate.

Traditional English cooking could also be found in pubs but with one or two notable exceptions they, too, have surrendered to Caesar salad, pesto risotto and New Zealand Sauvignon. So, to find cooking which is still hanging on to its roots, you'd better go to France or, if you take my advice, to Italy.

'I have prepared my peace,' Yeats wrote, 'with learned Italian things'. Italian things, not necessarily learned, must be part of any sensible last will and testament. The English need Italy as gardens need the sun. It can teach us how to live with our history, to find drama in everyday life and lighten our national tendency to gloom. It was always so. From the nineteenth century our greatest writers, from Byron to Browning to D.H. Lawrence, fled to Italy, and all tourists there were known as 'Inglese', regardless of their country of origin. So a Florentine hotelier was heard to say, 'I've got ten Inglese in tonight, four are French, four German and two Russian.' Harold Acton, wholly dedicated to Italy, told me that Pen Browning, the Brownings' son, was 'extremely interested in fornication' and so the bars and restaurants around Florence are peopled by direct descendants of the Barretts of Wimpole Street.

Every Italian city had not only its own history but also its own masterpiece in the cathedral, its own food, its own wine and often its own language. The Neapolitan dialect is incomprehensible to the pure-speaking Florentine. You wouldn't expect to eat spaghetti with clams in Bologna or wild boar pâté in Naples. If you want a town where the present and the past are still vividly alive, go to Siena. It's divided into parishes, which compete in the extraordinary horse-race round the scallop-shell-shaped piazza twice a year. The Palio, which celebrates a victory over rival Florence, takes only a few minutes but the preparations and the processions are unforgettable. The horses spend the previous night in local churches, to which they are led by men singing, and if they manure the marble floors it's a sign of luck. The long procession before the race, with parishioners in medieval costume throwing twirling flags into the air as high as the houses, unwinds slowly. Knights in armour, with their visors down, ride by to celebrate the parishes that no longer exist. Finally the Palio itself, a huge silver dish, is driven round on a cart drawn by white oxen. The secret ambition of all the parishes is not to win (winning entails a great deal of expense) but to have their enemy come second — a true humiliation.

The Palio has more importance than even the beauty of the event in Europe's most perfect city centre. Loyalty to your parish is so great that women giving birth in a hospital outside their home area take a little tray of earth from their home parish to put under the bed. And the parishes organize events, football matches, parties and dinners for young and old, rich and poor, all the year round. The system works so well that there is little juvenile crime in Siena. It should certainly be tried in Birmingham, preferably with a colourful horse-race round the Bull Ring.

Italian communists, who are about as far to the left as English Liberals, have done well in the preservation of Siena; but I must warn you about a deterioration in the Communist Party. One of the greatest pleasures you can look forward to in the summer is the outdoor opera in front of the cathedral in San Gimignano, the city of tall towers and Ghirlandaio. The former communist mayor wore Armani suits, drove a Mercedes, had a most elegant wife and always got us front-row seats at the opera, and occasional champagne. Sadly he has retired, and the present communist mayor wears trousers that might have come from Marks & Spencer and drives something like a Fiat Uno. He failed to provide us with champagne or front-row seats, so we detected a decline in the standards of Italian communism. Nothing has deteriorated, however, in the joy of watching the dusk turn to darkness and the moon rising as Rigoletto's tragedy unfolds, or hearing *Tosca* sung to an accompaniment of wailing car alarms in the neighbouring streets.

There is no deterioration either in the restaurant I'll leave to you. You must cross the Piazza del Campo in Siena and find a narrow street at the side of the Palazzo Pubblico. A little way up this street is Le Logge. You can sit outside it next to the façade of a Renaissance church, opposite the houses where the young are shouting down from bedroom windows and the old are sitting in chairs outside the front doors to enjoy the endless drama of the streets. As the motor bicycles whip by, a music student on holiday plays the flute and wandering refugees try to sell you erotic cigarette lighters. Or you can eat inside in an elegant nineteenth-century room which looks like the Café Momus in *La Bohème*. You can eat malfatti, a sort of pasta rarely met elsewhere, and drink the wine Gianni and Laura, who own the place, produce on their vineyards near Montalcino.

We are often in Italy with Ann Mallalieu and her husband, Tim Cassell, both lawyers but, whereas she is a Labour member of the House of Lords, he is full of charm and way to the right, not only of Genghis Khan but of Tony Blair and Margaret Thatcher. Some years ago Ann was defending a number of gay sadomasochists who, although harmless to others, found pleasure in nailing each other's genitalia to wooden boards in the privacy of an airport

214

hotel. It was Tim asking his wife, as barristers will, 'When's your penis torture beginning, darling?' that caused a great many heads to turn as we sat having our pre-dinner drinks in the Piazza del Campo.

Gianni invited us all to lunch in a house near to their vineyard. We sat down at a long table under the vines with all their friends, relations and waiters. After a good many bottles of wine, our hosts began to sing, quietly at first and then with growing fervour, *'Ciao, bella, oh! Ciao, bella, oh ciao bella, oh ciao, ciao, ciao.'* Our friend Tim joined in lustily, smiling and happy until I told him that what he was singing was a song of the communist resistance, at which point he stopped singing with an expression almost as pained as though he had been nailed up in some airport hotel.

26

The Pursuit of Happiness

It's as hard for a writer to describe happiness as it is to create a totally good character. Most of Shakespeare's comedies and many of his tragedies end with the re-establishment of a normal, peaceful and happy existence. But that's a state he carefully avoids writing about because it wouldn't be particularly good theatre. When happiness breaks out on the stage it is time to ring down the curtain. Henry James spoke for many writers when he referred to the 'bread sauce of the happy ending'. If happiness doesn't make good theatre, is it something to be actively pursued in life?

On the whole politicians don't think so. They have achieved greater fame by offering us blood, tears and sweat, saying grimly, 'Today the struggle,' and recommending death on the barricades or the battlefield as a more exciting option. Religions have also, by and large, taken a pretty grim view of existence.

The Greek gods, it's true, seemed capable of enjoying a good time. They may have been wilful, jealous, temperamental and frequently uncaring, but they were at least interested in sex and would take the trouble to transform themselves into various animals in the pursuit of love. For mere mortals, moments of sun-soaked delight, and the excitement of the Dionysian revels, were forever overshadowed by darker fears and terrors. On account of some, perhaps unconscious, crime or inherited shortcoming, the Furies would pursue you relentlessly and to the ends of the earth.

Christianity offered happiness beyond the grave, but it has been less encouraging during what Noël Coward said he believed in, 'life before death'. The way to heaven is often portrayed as hard and stony, demanding self-sacrifice, confession of sins, begging forgiveness, even martyrdom before receiving the final reward. Religions have prescribed penitence, pilgrimages or holy wars. There has been, among the faithful, very little talk of enjoying a thoroughly good time.

I suppose that the idea of humanity's right to happiness started at the time of the

American Declaration of Independence, which as far as I can discover was the first document which held the truth to be self-evident that all men are endowed with certain inalienable rights, among which were 'life, and liberty, and the pursuit of happiness'. In spite of worries about wealth, diet, terrorism, eating too much salt, taking exercise and failing to conform to the company's image, most Americans do feel, I'm sure, that happiness is worth pursuing. The English are resigned to its being as incalculable, and perhaps as disappointing, as the weather.

Is the idea of happiness an entirely human invention? Animals are contented when they are feeding or asleep, a condition dogs enjoy most of the time. When they're awake and going about their business, they seem usually nervous, peering about them for signs of danger and taking sudden fright. Horses shy at a blown newspaper, a footstep in the woods sends rooks clattering up to the sky, rabbits panicking and deer cantering into the darkness of closer trees, deeper undergrowth. As Shelley knew, human beings also find moments of contentment suddenly filled with anxiety, which sends us scurrying away into the shadows:

We look before and after;
We pine for what is not;
Our sincerest laughter
With some pain is fraught.

At high moments of love, how many men are looking furtively at their watches behind some tousled head and thinking, It's time I was back in the office? How many women are wondering how on earth they got involved with a person who keeps his socks on? At the liveliest restaurant dinner, someone is worrying about the bill. On the most idyllic beaches there is a general concern about flies, mosquitoes, where the children have got to now or how to make conversation for a whole week with a partner who's usually at work all day and sleeps in front of the television at night. Like nervous animals, our natural state is one of anxiety.

We worry about most things, and then worry about worrying, or worry if we suddenly find there's nothing much to worry about. And if you've got nothing to worry about, the government will oblige by starting a war, for instance, or telling you that the streets are about to be taken over by violent and abusive beggars. Politicians are in desperate need of fear and anxiety in order that they may appear to be the only persons who can steer us safely through these dangers.

I can only suggest you do your best to banish anxiety, possibly with a glass of champagne, and lay yourself open to the moment when happiness becomes irresistible. I'm writing this at a good time of the year. The beech trees are covered with fresh, green leaves — we are going to have a birthday lunch in the garden. My grandchildren will play in the mysterious sunken copses, disused flint pits now filled with tall and ancient trees, where I also played as a child. The daffodils will be in flower and the dogs will be jumping over them. There is every possible reason for happiness; but it's also a moment of sadness too. How many more such birthdays will there be? It's sad my mother never saw Rosie and Emily, my daughters, grow up. Although Shelley was right about our sincerest laughter being fraught with sadness, it's the sadness, in a way, which makes happiness complete.

There is a story about a devoted fisherman, in love with the sport, who went to sleep and found himself, on a perfect day, fishing in a clear stream. Every time he cast he hooked a fine salmon. After this had happened a dozen times in succession he asked the gillie where he was. Was it, perhaps, heaven? No, he was told, it's hell. Happiness too often or too regularly repeated becomes misery. And here perhaps we're getting near to what happiness is for me. Happiness is a by-product. If it's sought for deliberately, desperately, it's elusive and often deceptive, like the distant sight of an oasis. If you aim to live a life that is eventful, interesting, exciting, even though it's bound to be also disappointing, frustrating and with inevitable moments of despair, happiness may, from time to time, unexpectedly turn up.

When I was a child I was stage-struck. Now I only have to go into an empty auditorium to see a rehearsal, or even those draughty, dusty, church halls where the seats are indicated with marker tape on the floor and the actors are drinking instant coffee out of paper cups, to find excitement, a flow of adrenalin, a happiness and an expectation that I suppose some people get from robbing banks. That's the moment of happiness which usually gets to its high point in the final rehearsal. From then on it's downhill, the piece is done and then shown, and alas the public are let in. Anxiety mounts, worries take over — will they, won't they, like it? The gloom lifts gradually, normal life returns and you prepare for another moment of happiness and another exposure to disaster.

And for writers, certainly for barristers after they have won cases, and, I imagine, for surgeons after a successful operation and architects after the building has gone up, there is greater happiness in finishing things. This happiness is also of course combined with some feeling of loss. I think it has been best described by Edward Gibbon, who speaks of the moment of triumph when he laid down his pen, having completed *The Decline and Fall of the Roman Empire*: 'But my pride was soon humbled, and a sober melancholy spread over my mind, by the idea that I had taken an everlasting leave of an old and agreeable companion.'

And happiness can take you over completely and without regret at the most unexpected and apparently inappropriate moments. Basingstoke was once a pleasant country town, but soulless new buildings and gigantic office blocks have made it drearily unattractive. I was performing in the theatre there and, because the dressing room was down a long flight of stairs, they fixed me up with somewhere to change in a small paint shop at the side of the stage. The sink was full of paintbrushes, paint-stained newspapers littered the floor, the walls were decorated with old saws and various tools, and there was, of course, no loo. One of the actresses I was performing with found me a bucket.

So there was I on a wet Sunday evening, peeing into a bucket in a small paint shop beside a stage in Basingstoke. It suddenly occurred to me, much to my surprise, that I was completely happy.

27

Looking after Your Health

I have to confess that when a doctor asked me if I found myself out of breath when taking exercise, I had to say, 'How would I know? I've never taken exercise.'

Exercise has become, in my lifetime, the modern form of prayer. When religious belief faltered, and faith in immortality and an afterlife free of any kind of physical disability faded, it became essential to prolong a healthy life on earth by all available means. Gyms, saunas and swimming pools took the place of churches and chapels. A little sports bag slung over the shoulder took the place of hymn books and missals as the faithful passed to their devotions. The father confessor was replaced by the personal trainer; voices once raised in hymns are now united in the muted drone of the yoga class and the muttered counting of swimming-pool lengths.

It's hard to say if these new religious rituals bring as much joy to the congregations as older forms of religion and it's difficult to know exactly how effective they are. You seldom see a happy, even a cheerful-looking, jogger and it's often said that the only people who lose weight from massage are the masseurs, who sweat away, kneading bulging stomachs or inflated bottoms. However that may be, and as with the older religious observances, it's not the immediately obvious results that matter but the assertion of faith in a better life to come.

I don't particularly want to hand my atheistical prejudices on to those who will come after me. It's true that the word 'gym' has always been associated in my mind with smelly plimsolls, cold showers, daunting vaulting horses, ropes I couldn't climb and unnecessary dashes to the top of the wall bars. 'Taking exercise' at school always meant for me changing into shorts and then hiding in the loo behind the squash court with a good book. I don't mean to recommend a total disbelief in the worship of health, but to inspire, perhaps, a little agnosticism.

No one could ever wish you a painful illness, a shortened life or a serious disability. The complaints I inherited, asthma and glaucoma, are enough of an inconvenience. And yet you may find some minor ailment, a disability you can learn to live with, could have its advantages. If one of your legs gives up the struggle against old age, you can experience the pleasure and privilege of a wheelchair at airports and be drawn, like an emperor on his chariot, through the struggling crowds to be taken first on to the plane. At JFK you will be driven in a further triumph past the half-a-mile-long queue of travellers waiting to have their passports stamped, to be whisked through with the minimum amount of fuss.

Failing eyesight has also proved useful and there are moments when it's a help to reduce the world around you to a comforting blur. When I was briefed in obscenity cases, it was part of our duty to watch the blue movies we were defending put on by the sergeant in charge of the projector at Scotland Yard. To actually see these entertainments was likely to put you off sex, at least until next Thursday. To protect myself against this affliction I used to take off my glasses and the picture was then reduced to a formless pink blur. I was spared the pain of one defendant who, at his trial, begged the judge to send him down to the cells so that he might not have to watch the stuff he sold. 'No,' said the merciless and hard-hearted judge, 'you'll sit in the dock and watch every second of it!'

Moderate deafness can also have its advantages. If you are known to be hard of hearing you obviously haven't heard inconvenient remarks or instructions. Evelyn Waugh derived great pleasure and assistance from his ear trumpet. When a conversation at dinner bored him he would merely lower it and retreat into merciful silence and contemplation.

Another advantage of the minor disability is that it provides fresh conversational openings as an alternative to the weather or the war. People can say, 'How's the leg?' and feel they have done you a kindness, which you needn't repay by telling them. Long ago I knew an elderly barrister healthy and quite free from pain, who had an imaginary complaint which he called 'my old trouble'. 'How are you, Hugh?' people used to say to him, and he'd answer, 'Perfectly all right, apart from my "old trouble", of course.' 'Well, how is the old trouble?' 'Much as always, I'm afraid.' This 'old trouble' saved him from dinner parties ('I'd love to of course, but the old trouble's been playing me up in the evenings lately'), holidays he didn't want to go on, or cases he felt sure he'd lose. I merely mention it in passing, but an 'old trouble' is something you may find extremely useful as the years go by.

28

Inventions and the
Decline of Language

During my lifetime inventions have fallen upon us as thick and fast as cluster bombs in some war against terrorism, with the intention of destabilizing the civilian population. Life, let us say between the publication of *David Copperfield* and *Mrs Dalloway*, didn't change enormously. But since then it has altered greatly due to a proliferation of inventions. It's as hard to think of Virginia Woolf surfing the Internet, or walking with a mobile phone clamped to her ear, riding an exercise bicycle, watching a DVD or sending a text message as it is to think of the Duke of Wellington in a jeep or Shakespeare with a word processor.

It's tempting to wonder how many of the inventions of the past century we might have been better off without. Take the aeroplane, for instance. It has transformed warfare from an event in which trained soldiers kill each other on distant battlefields to occasions when death is rained down indiscriminately on innocent civilians, while the professional fighters fly at a great height in comparative safety.

I can remember the train journeys to the South of France in my childhood, asleep in a dark mahogany compartment, dinner under the pink-shaded lights of the restaurant car, waking up at three in the morning to the clatter of newspaper trolleys on Lyons station and going back to sleep, until you woke up again to bright sunlight on the olive groves. Perhaps it's only the memories of childhood which make it seem a better experience than sitting, vaguely terrified, as a tubular machine bumps and rattles its way through the clouds offering you plastic food and no view of the countryside.

All right, it's no doubt far too late to do without the aeroplane, but did we ever need the mobile phone? Watch the crowds go by, one hand pressed to the side of their heads as though they are all suffering from a powerful earache, muttering incessantly to other marchers in other crowds clasping their hands to the side of their faces. The climax to the widespread use of the new technology came when a man was seen relieving himself in the Gents of a London hotel. One hand held his member and directed his stream, with the other he was expertly sending a text message on his mobile phone. Once people sat still to make phone calls. Now the summons of some particularly maddening little tune is the cue for a walk round the garden or a heaven-sent opportunity to start making a cheese soufflé with the free hand. It's doubtful if this invention has added much to the sum total of human happiness.

Then there is computer technology, an invention that throws off such a strong atmosphere of sexual allure that it makes our leaders feel young, up to date, thrusting and in touch, and in schools learning to manipulate these devices seems to have crowded out lessons in history, literature and music. My first thought about computers was that they slowed down communication considerably. Take getting into a hotel room, for instance. In my youth you arrived and the receptionist looked in a book, ticked something with a pen, unhooked a key and you were in. Now you're met with a puzzled girl whose name is on a little plaque pinned to her lapel. She starts to play the computer like a bewildered and

uncertain composer in search of a tune —
a considerable time passes and various
chords are struck and discord often follows. Once I was allocated a room in a part
of the hotel that hadn't yet been built.

No doubt you can get reams of information from computers, and find out all
about Einstein, Gérard de Nerval and
cheap air tickets, and you can work from
home. There lies the greatest danger. Soon
office life will be a thing of the past, everyone will stay at home all day, peering at
screens and communicating by e-mail,
often irritating their husbands and wives or
partners, who long for the days when they
were out of the way by seven thirty in the
morning. There will be an end to office ro-
mances, kisses snatched in the postroom
and the fascinating plots and counter-plots
of office politics. Lonely workers at home
will remember with nostalgia the happy
days of catching the eight fifteen to Water-
loo.

We might ask the scientists of our time
to give it a rest, take a long holiday and
stop inventing things for at least another
half a century. It's important to remember
that all these ingenious ways of sending
messages have no importance in themselves. The 'medium is the message' is one

of the world's silliest remarks. The message is the message, and it doesn't matter whether you send it by e-mail, a note in a bottle or on a picture postcard. The book, or the poem, or the play is what counts and it doesn't matter if it's written with a pen on a long sheet of ruled paper, as I am writing now, or on the most highly developed word processor. No machine can help with the rhythms of your prose, even if it can spell better than you can.

Whether or not it's the fault of information technology, there has been an extraordinary deterioration in our language, at least as it's spoken by the governing classes. Words have been reduced to letters so they can fit on to a text message, and such invitations as CU4T are moderately entertaining; but in general the technological age has resulted in our language becoming divorced from grammar, growing curiously inflated and getting lost in the sort of meaningless haze that affects the directions for assembling furniture bought in parts.

Nouns like 'access', 'source' and 'task' now reappear as verbs. You can 'access' almost anything, from the refrigerator to directory inquiries. The jargon has even spread to the theatre, where new dramas get regularly 'workshopped' before audiences 'access' them. So I might 'source' a play and 'task' someone to 'workshop' it. Among the more ludicrous titles invented for government officials we are now to have an 'access regulator' who will see who gets into university. The phrase could be equally applied to a lift attendant.

This is Beverley Hughes, a government minister, as quoted by Matthew Parris in *The Times.* She is talking, although you might not notice the fact, about identity cards:

'I think an entitlement card could offer some important contributions both to the challenges we face and also to some important new concepts that we're trying to introduce to this issue around entitlement and also around citizenship, but the most important thing is that we actually stimulate debate, a widespread debate, among ordinary people, and I think, I *hope* that because we have actually, genuinely tried to bring a really fresh look and some creative thinking to the debate, that I hope people will be, I hope, pleasantly surprised by the document; it's very comprehensive, it looks at all the issues for and against, and the important thing, as I say, is that we want to hear the voices of ordinary people.'

This has every misuse of language to which politicians are prone, including avoiding the words 'identity card', which sounds like the engine of a fascist dictatorship, and calling the same thing an 'entitlement card', which sounds as though you've won something. This is the hope behind changing the word 'refugees', which makes us feel sorry for fugitives from some tyranny, to 'asylum seekers', which seems to describe awkward people who are always trying to get something for nothing. We can no longer use the word 'unemployed' because unemployment has, of course, been abolished, so we have to talk about 'job seekers'. To call the unfriendly act of shooting your own side 'friendly fire' or the death of innocent civilians 'collateral damage' is equally cowardly and inane.

It is, of course, totally unfair but nevertheless instructive to compare Beverely Hughes to Queen Elizabeth I. You might say that they are both politicians, but Elizabeth lived at a time when you didn't seem to be able to open your mouth without speaking beautifully, whereas Beverley is of a generation that has seen our language reach the point of collapse. I don't know how long it took Elizabeth to work out what she was going to say to the fleet at Tilbury. Perhaps she did it off the cuff. I'm quite sure she didn't read her speech off a piece of paper with her head down. 'I know I have the body of a weak and feeble woman,' she said, 'but I have the heart and stomach of a king, and of a king of England too; and I think foul scorn that Parma or Spain, or any prince of Europe, should dare to invade the borders of my realm.'

It isn't only the highly educated monarch in the distant past who can still teach us how our language can be clearly and beautifully used. The 'Notable British Trials' series is full of memorable phrases used by those convicted of serious crimes. Armstrong, a Welsh solicitor, handing a poisoned scone to an intended victim, politely said, 'Excuse fingers'. Edith Thompson, an incurable romantic, a sort of Madame Bovary of Wanstead Park, was in love with a young seaman called Frederick Bywaters, whom, so it was said, she induced to stab her husband to death. One of her love letters to Bywaters is, I think, a fine example of the plain, simple but moving use of our language:

It was rather fun on Thursday at the Garden Party. They had swings and roundabouts and flipflaps, coconut shies, Aunt Sallies, Hoopla and all that sort of thing. I went in for them all and shocked a lot of people, I think. I didn't care though. I'd got a rather posh frock on, a white georgette with rows and rows of jade ribbon and white fur and large white hat, but all that didn't deter me from going into a fried fish shop in Snaresbrook and buying fish and chips. Getting it home was the worst part — it absolutely smelt the bus out. I didn't mind — it was rather fun — only I wished you had been with me. I think two halves would have enjoyed themselves, better than one half by herself.

Goodbye, for now, darlingest pal.

Edith Thompson and her lover were both hanged in 1923. The Court of Appeal said it was 'rather an ordinary sort of case'. Perhaps she died because she was too much in love, and expressed it too well.

29

Avoiding Utopia

A map of the world which doesn't contain Utopia, Oscar Wilde said, is not worth looking at. While I think it's admirable to have Utopia on your map and that you can keep it in mind, even set off in what you imagine to be its direction, there must be no serious danger of your ever reaching it. Utopia, should it exist, might be like the common view of heaven, with absolutely nothing to complain about. Boredom in Utopia might soon set in because there would be no more to try for.

All the same, many people have described Utopia, from Thomas More to William Morris. In Samuel Butler's *Erewhon* (an anagram of nowhere), criminals are sent to hospital and the sick to prisons, an idea which has a superficial attraction but one which might not be entirely practical. In the real world attempts to produce Utopian societies have had, on the whole, disastrous results.

Russia during the Stalin era was no doubt more like hell than heaven, a place of terror rather than a just city. But Russia in the time of glasnost, the early Gorbachev years and the end of the Afghan war seemed to many people a refuge from the shallow and monetarist West. It was a country with a blessed absence of advertisements, where everyone on the Underground had their heads stuck in *War and Peace* or the translations of Dickens and J.B. Priestley, where the workers went to the ballet, where Chekhov and Gogol were seen as gods and the population spent its leisure hours cultivating the deep resources of the Russian soul.

I first met Gorbachev's Russia when I went to Moscow with our National Theatre. It was a tour of Shakespeare's three great last plays of reconciliation and forgiveness. There were minor inconveniences of course. I was shown into a hotel bedroom only to find two men in crumpled blue suits lying on the bed, watching television and eating pickled cucumbers out of a plastic bag. They were extremely reluctant to move, and I had to unpack and even start to undress before they finally left. One of the actors was less lucky.

He came back late from the theatre to find a man asleep in his bed. When he complained to the stern-faced woman at the end of the corridor, she only gave an uncaring laugh and put up a small camp bed beside his unknown companion. Breakfast might take a couple of hours to come, but Muscovite friends would invite you to their houses and set out every piece of ham and cheese, every drop of vodka they still had in their cupboard, for your entertainment. Caviare and champanski were cheap at the National Hotel if you could pay by Barclaycard.

Emily was learning Russian at school and she became fluent in the language on her first visit, when she fell in love with a Russian poet. It was he who led her across Red Square in the moonlight, with the red lights twinkling over the Kremlin, and told her it was an extraordinary honour to be walking across Red Square hand in hand 'with a girl whose father defended the Sex Pistols . . .' I found it to be a general rule that the children of reasonably well-off, middle-class homes fell in love with the soulfulness of Russia. Those with more working-class backgrounds found that it stood for everything they were determined to get away from and hated it. Peter Hall, the theatre's multi-talented director, left suddenly by train for England after the oppressive Moscow reminded him too painfully of his childhood before he got into Cambridge and became a star.

But even then, in Moscow, where the ideal Utopian city was still only a distant shape on the map, I remember talking to the chain-smoking director of the Moscow Art Theatre, who was lamenting the lack of any new writers to replace not only Chekhov and Turgenev but the lesser-known authors who managed, in subtle ways, to ridicule the Party tyranny. 'They used to shake the bars of the cage,' he said, 'and that gave them their strength. Now the cage no longer has bars, they can walk about freely and they don't know where to go.' This was an unusual argument for censorship, and another warning against the discovery of Utopia.

So we moved on to Tbilisi, which is less like Utopia and more like Naples, and the Georgians, who gave birth to Stalin, think less about their souls than drinking endless toasts and persuading girls to make love at first sight. One of the actresses, wandering through the town, was accosted by a man who said, 'You have very nice breasts and I know a quiet square where we can make love immediately.'

The lorries containing the scenery and costumes broke down on the road from Moscow so that the three last plays had to be performed by actors in jeans and T-shirts, using rulers for swords. This made them look even more wonderful, but we wondered why we ever thought there was, during the Cold War, any serious danger of Russia conquering the world when they couldn't deliver the scenery for *The Tempest.*

I next visited the country some thought of as Utopia when Emily was spending a year in Moscow as part of her course at university. The soul was not, by then, the only concern of the Russians, nor did its study provide their main occupation. A big and beautiful art deco hotel near Red Square had been restored to become one of the most expensive in Europe. Having booked a table there with some difficulty, I had to feign a sudden heart attack when I saw the prices on the menu and take refuge back in the old National Hotel.

Life, however, had become easier. Great jars of caviare, duck, pork chops and Georgian wine were available for a few dollars in the market. We didn't have to take taxis (the statue of Lenin with his hand raised is said to have caught him in a vain attempt to stop a Moscow taxi). Emily walked into the middle of the road to stop any passing car which would postpone its original journey and take us to wherever we wanted to go for a few more dollars. I have seen, to my horror, Muscovites divert ambulances and even fire engines in this way.

Emily's first love, her Russian poet, still seemed to stand for the old soulful days although their romance was over. He took us to the Writers' Union, beautifully housed in the building Tolstoy used as the Rostov mansion in *War and Peace*. When we'd first gone there it had, in fact, contained many writers. Now there were as many businessmen talking on their mobile phones. Our poet fetched bottles of variously flavoured vodka from the cellar, read us his published poem for Emily and lamented the break-up of the Soviet Union. We got seriously drunk, remembering lost times.

But there were still great moments. Emily took a course at the Moscow Art Theatre, and I watched her teacher recite Pushkin with a cigarette dangling from his lower lip. We stocked up with food from the market and had a party in Emily's flat. The place was filled with actors, some sang and one mimed the dilemma of a hunter who, with a fat bird in the sights of his gun, had an irresistible urge to visit the lavatory. There was something of soul left.

More recently Emily went back to Russia, wanting to find Stanislavsky's house and undertake further research for a book about Olga Knipper, Chekhov's wife. Her poet met her at the airport and suggested they retire to the lavatory to smoke dope and then have lunch at the Pizza Hut. Moscow, where the streets and subways were once the safest in the world, is now a city of rapes and muggings, and automatic rifles can be bargained for and bought in the kiosks which once sold sweets and magazines or, occasionally, a single shoe.

Emily went to find Stanislavsky's house, where Chekhov, writing in the garden, heard the distant sound of a little train that was reproduced in *The Cherry Orchard*. All she found was an empty field with a small notice telling visitors that Stanislavsky's house was once there. Travelling further, she found, still standing, the home of Nemirovich-Danchenko, Stanislavsky's and Chekhov's great inspirer at the Moscow Art Theatre. The house was full of workmen who had been sent to repair it but, never having been paid, couldn't get back to Moscow. Utopia was finally off the map, or it had been converted to the everyday world of crime, poverty and the doubtful values of the marketplace.

Communism and Christianity, it's been said, are the two great Utopian ideals, and we don't really know if they'd work because they've never been tried. Much the same thing can be said about democracy, which Western states, believing they have come nearer to Utopia than the darker tyrannies of the Third World, claim as their great glory and the solution to all political problems.

I suppose democracy was most nearly achieved in ancient Greece, when everyone except women and slaves took part in the government. The result was usually disastrous and led to the death of Socrates, just as the introduction of democracy in England would lead to the restoration of hanging, which the majority of the population favour. Far from having government by the people and for the people, in England we hand over what amounts to absolute power to the leader of the party with the majority of seats in Parliament. Far from the people having a say in government, the present Prime Minister has involved us in a war that most people didn't want when it started. France and Germany, whose governments obeyed their people's wish to have no part in the war, are abused as traitors to the cause of peace and democratic rule.

You should be wary of Members of Parliament who claim special wisdom and the right to power because they are 'democratically elected'. At periodic elections we vote for the party we have always supported and the leader who most appeals to us. Nowadays, when the hustings have fallen silent and barracking has gone out of style, few people can remember, or perhaps have ever heard, the name of their local MP unless he's a member of the government or appears on television. It's noticeable that the House of Lords, where, at the moment, no one is elected by the public, has on the whole more interesting and better-informed debates and is far more active in protecting civil rights against the brutal assaults perpetrated by Labour home secretaries who represent the party that won the election. Perhaps the House of Lords, as it is at present constituted, is attractive because, as Lord Melbourne said of the Order of the Garter, 'There's no damned merit about it.'

Our system, which we call democracy, at

least leaves us the right from time to time to get rid of those who wish to govern us. And, if it's nowhere near Utopia, it is probably the best of all imperfect systems. All I can do is to advise you to be very cautious of those who claim to represent you and order you about for your own good.

Oscar Wilde, who knew Bernard Shaw and went to meetings of the Fabian Society, had socialism on his Utopian map. The great advantage of such a system, he thought, was that you would no longer have to endure the pain of feeling pity for the poor and the oppressed and could happily devote yourself to life and art with a clear conscience. It's an attractive argument and might be more persuasive if socialist governments had been more successful in putting an end to poverty and oppression.

It was in his life, in spite of all its imperfections and misfortunes, rather than in his political beliefs, that Wilde showed the true sweetness of his nature. His friend Oswald Sickert had died and his widow had shut herself away in her room, inconsolable, and refused to see anyone. Wilde called at the house but Nellie Sickert, her daughter, told him her mother wouldn't see him. When the mother repeatedly called out, 'Send him away,' from behind a locked door, Wilde said he'd stay in the house until she opened it to him. Finally she did and he was admitted to her room. Nellie Sickert waited downstairs for the inevitable inconsolable tears.

There was a long silence and then, incredibly, she heard a strange and unexpected sound. It was her mother laughing. Wilde had charmed her, cheered her, amused her and brought her back to life. Perhaps in that moment he got nearer to Utopia than all the political systems ever thought of or looked for on maps.

30

Fires Were Started

One of my heroes has always been Prometheus, chained to a rock, his liver pecked out by the birds every day and restored for further torture each night — and all for conferring one of the greatest benefits on mankind. He gave back fire to us after the king of the gods, an unreliable character with dubious morals, had withdrawn it. Prometheus tricked the Olympians into eating merely the bones and fat of the beasts sacrificed to them. He also described that yawning gap which still exists between us and our gods.

Thanks to Prometheus, fire played a great part in my childhood. We had a daily ceremony, during school holidays, of burning the rubbish to the accompaniment of 'You're the cream in my coffee' played on a wind-up gramophone. We would light fires in one of the two copses in the garden and cook sausages, or bake potatoes in the dying embers, pulling them out with sticks, blowing off the grey ash and eating them with butter.

One of the few advantages of my public-school education was the fireplace in our rooms. You could not only make toast but start a self-taught cooking course with, say, an occasional mushroom omelette. In those extraordinary days the butler, whose name was George, would appear in your room and, Zeus-like, rake out the fire with a poker, say, 'Good night, sir,' and shut us down for the night. It was my difficult room-mate Tainton who heated the poker handle until it was just red hot and left it out in the hope that George would seize it and burn off several fingers. George knew exactly what was going on. He used Tainton's best Sunday trousers as a readily available poker holder and burned a large hole in the seat.

Forget Proust's little cake, for me there is no smell more reminiscent of childhood than leaves burning in the autumn, and the place of the fire in the garden, behind the frames and the small greenhouse, has always been a source of great pleasure. Christmas and birthdays are especially welcome because of the vast amounts of wrapping paper to be burned. At other

250

times you have to make do with the 'Business', 'Money' and 'Sports' sections of the heavyweight newspapers. Add to these the usual household rubbish, the mass of uninvited faxes and half of each morning's post and you can get a blaze which sends sparks into the trees and lights up the cabbages.

Of course I have had accidents. For some reason I put a pair of tailor-made trousers, my braces and a short-wave radio into a cardboard box in order to carry them downstairs. At the end of my session with the bonfire, I heard a faint murmuring, a voice, possibly speaking in a foreign language, uttering a vague complaint among the ashes. It was what remained of the short-wave radio. Further investigation revealed the metal parts of the braces. It was a misfortune, but slight and bearable when you compare it to what happened to Prometheus.

Am I, then, a closet pyromaniac? Possibly. There was one unpleasant judge down at the Old Bailey who, when sentencing arsonists, always alleged that setting fire to things caused such offenders to experience an orgasm. I can honestly say that lighting a fire has never had this result so far as I'm concerned. To me a satisfactory fireplace is a sign of peace, happiness and good will, as it was for Dickens when the fires lit up and warmed the Christmases at Dingly Dell. Scrooge's miserliness was proved by the fact that he allowed only one coal on his clerk's fire, and kept the coal box locked in his own room. A roaring fire is the Dickensian sign of generosity.

One of the many advantages of the hotel we stay in in Morocco is the fire in the bedrooms. The logs are dry, dead wood from the orange groves and cork trees. On the whole they burn easily but there is some degree of skill required in building them into a little pyramid which you can light with a single sheet of the *Daily Telegraph* someone has brought over on the plane. With its help, and a few twigs from the lemon tree outside the window, you can start what the French-speaking Moroccans call *'une bonne cheminée'*. Arabs who live in hot countries are always fearful of the cold, wearing sweaters and thick socks under their djellabas and being expert on keeping log fires going. There are few pleasures to beat going to bed with big logs in the *'cheminée'* reading a little and then switching off the lamp to go to sleep by flickering firelight.

Back in England there are too many

empty grates, although there are still unexpected delights. I did a week of performances at the King's Head, a pub theatre in Islington. To my delight there was a coal fire in my dressing room and there were two young assistant directors, who had majored in theatre studies, to keep it going throughout the evening.

At home I can stop work around six o'clock and find happiness in the sitting room with a packet of firelighters and a box of matches. There's a little anxiety before our logs, heavy with rain and sap, unlike the quick-burning wood of Morocco, start to burn; but then there's a lot to watch. 'Pictures in the fire' they used to call it in my childhood; the pictures are what you choose to make of them, but in any event, it's far more interesting than sitting looking at a radiator.

Don Giovanni, who, like Prometheus, refused to repent and so became a hero in the Romantic age, was dragged down to the fires of hell. At least, I have always thought, they must be warmer than the cold and marmoreal corridors of heaven. Even if neither of these places are found to exist, you can guess what I want done with my body when the time comes to read out my will. At least the grave needn't be cold.

31

A Writer's Life

'You speak of fame, of happiness, of a glorious, interesting life and to me all these nice words, pardon me, are just like Turkish delight which I never eat.'

So says Trigorin, the moderately successful writer in Chekhov's play *The Seagull*, and he goes on to describe the writer's perpetual guilt: 'Day and night I am overwhelmed by one besetting idea: I must write, I must write, I must write. I have scarcely finished one long story when I must somehow start another, then a third, after that a fourth . . .'

It's true that guilt follows a writer wherever he goes, an unnecessarily faithful dog, always yapping at his heels. When bank managers, surgeons, garage mechanics or head waiters go on holiday to Minorca or the Amalfi coast, their work stays at home; the bank, the operating theatre, the garage or the restaurant doesn't accompany them in their hand baggage. Work would be impossible for them, at least for a carefree fortnight. But for a writer work is never impossible; the pen and the notebook, or, I suppose, even the laptop, are always with him, and can be brought out in any hotel lounge, café, train or aeroplane. A writer never has an excuse for not working. If any of you think of taking up the business, you will have to remember that the world is full of blank sheets of paper waiting to be filled, and endless hours in which you should have completed your daily thousand words. 'I write ceaselessly, as though travelling post haste, and I can't do otherwise,' Trigorin goes on. 'Where's the splendour and glory in that, I ask you?'

With this burden of guilt to dispose of, I've found it best to start as early in the day as possible. 'Before I bath, shave or shit or anything like that,' was Graham Greene's programme for his daily routine number of words, which, inexorably, built up to a brilliant lifetime's work. However you time it, and starting at six a.m. seems to get harder as the years go by, it's best to get it done by lunchtime, before the first drink and the heavy-lidded afternoon; although you can pull yourself together at around five o'clock to correct what you wrote in the morning and feel, of course, dissatisfied with it.

All of this might seem a simple, even routine business, if a writer's only job were to write. I assume that you were born with an ear for prose or poetry, a gift for constructing sentences which catch the reader's attention, the ability to describe a scene or advance an argument which will seem truthful and surprising — but this is only half of it. A writer not only has to write, he has to live in order to have something to write about. And of the two occupations, living is much the hardest.

'I see a cloud resembling a piano' — Trigorin again — 'and I think I must mention [that] in a story . . . I catch a whiff of heliotrope. Immediately I register it in my mind: a cloying odour, a widow's flower, to be mentioned in a description of a summer evening. I catch you and myself up at every phrase . . . to lock up at once in my literary warehouse, it may come in useful.'

You can rely on childhood, a period when every endless afternoon, every corner of the garden, every night fear, moment of loneliness or rare triumph, seems brilliantly lit and clear in your memory. This part of life is every writer's free gift to start with; further experiences have to be worked at and, perhaps, suffered for.

Love, hope, disappointment, exultation and despair will no doubt come, even if uninvited. What you'll need is some knowledge of how other people behave at moments of crisis, how they talk, what avenues of retreat and concealment they discover, or with what unexpected bravery they deal with apparently impossible lives. For this purpose it's a great help to get a job which has nothing to do with writing but one in which as many people as possible are likely to confide in you. You might be a priest or a doctor or a social worker, a hairdresser or an agony aunt, or seek employment with a dating agency.

I count myself extremely lucky to have been called to the bar in my twenties and to have immediately found middle-aged women, businessmen and suburban housewives ready to pour out all the secrets of their lives. I was fortunate enough to meet murderers, con men, contract killers, politicians with unrevealed scandals and, on one horrible occasion, an assistant hangman. All of this was a great privilege and seems to me to have been more useful than moving, with the publication of my first novel — an event which happened shortly before I got called to the bar — into the world of editors, publishers and other writers. The bar exams are pretty dull, as is learning law academically when it's not connected with real human beings in trouble, but it's well worth it for the help you may get as a writer.

You will also have to face the fact that, as a writer, you will be a difficult if not a maddening person to live with. The writer is seldom entirely involved in any situation. Some part of him is standing aside, the detached observer, taking notes to store in his 'literary warehouse'. This is deeply frustrating to those in need of a fully committed love affair, or even a completely meaningful quarrel. On the rare occasions when I am in dispute with my wife, a partner in what is an unusually happy marriage, I am memorizing her dialogue so that I may give extracts from it to Hilda Rumpole in one of her many disagreements with her fictional husband.

The fact that writers are hard to live with is another good reason for getting a job where you'll meet real people and learn something of their secrets. 'You may become a writer,' my father told me when I had confessed my secret ambition. 'You might even become a moderately successful writer. But consider the horrible life your wife would lead if you were such a thing. Writers are at home all day, wearing a dressing gown, brewing tea, stumped for words. Choose a job which will get you out of the house, if only for the sake of your poor wife. Why don't you divorce a few people? It's not very difficult.' So, wisely he guided me towards the bar.

Getting to know people, living an eventful life with useful experiences, such tasks have to be faced, and can be performed by the writer. But there still remains a daunting question for the author of fiction. What on earth is the story?

Story-telling, it has to be admitted, has gone somewhat out of style. A plot has come to be considered a mechanical thing, unimportant compared to fine writing, startling but unconnected situations or a novel attitude to life. And yet a plot, a story, is what induced weary audiences to stay awake listening to Homer, or what still makes us turn the page or watch the unfolding of a play. Unless the reader, or the listener, wants to know what happens next, he or she quickly loses interest. Stories are therefore essential to the writer of fiction; but where they come from is often a mystery, and the great worry is that they may not come at all.

There is general agreement that the characters should create the plot, and that the plot shouldn't be there to create the characters. However, in his *Aspects of the Novel* E.M. Forster contemplated the embarrassing situation when wonderfully created characters refuse to bestir themselves to act out any scene of a story:

> In vain it (the plot) points out to those unwieldy creatures (the characters) the advantages of the triple process, complication, crisis, and solution so persuasively expounded by Aristotle. A few of them rise and comply . . . but there is no general response. They want to sit and brood or something. And the plot (which I here visualize as a sort of higher government official) is concerned at their lack of public spirit.

Every writer in search of a story must recognize this agony but I can't agree with Forster's dismissal of the plot as a sort of busybody bureaucrat. Hamlet, Lear and Othello have their characters revealed through the plots and counter-plots that concern them and we wouldn't have learned much about them if nothing had ever happened.

In a time when plots are considered to be of minor importance, it's still recognized that crime stories, tales of detection, can't do without them. For this reason crime writing is regarded, in some quarters, as a sort of inferior occupation, the popular musical compared to the grand opera of the serious novel. And yet much of the greatest literature could, in one sense, be described as crime writing. Aeschylus's *Agamemnon* and *Hamlet* are certainly crime stories. *Othello* is a story about the theft of a handkerchief. *Macbeth* deals with the unpleasant murder of a house guest, and the effect or non-effect of remorse after that crime has been committed. The works of Dickens, which are regarded as mainstream literature, depend greatly on crime. *Bleak House* produced a detective and *Great Expectations* depends on the introduction of a criminal very early in the proceedings. It has been suggested that the slow unfolding of a mystery that is known to the author but isn't exposed to the reader is the mark of a crime story. But again, *Great Expectations* is founded on a mystery that is not revealed until the conclusion of the book. All writers in all fields use mystery, suspense, the withholding of information, the puzzlement and the final enlightenment of the reader.

So when you have learned that a workable plot is not something confined to detective fiction, you have to look for a story and wonder, and this is certainly the hardest part of a writer's life, where on earth it might be discovered. Shakespeare got most of his plots from his comparatively small library of books and transformed them, but we are not Shakespeare. It has also been said that there are only a few basic stories in the world, *Cinderella* and *Blue Beard* both having given birth to numerous descendants, but even this thought may not comfort you. How can you make a fully developed, credible and yet surprising, revealing and mysterious story enter your head when it is needed? The answer is that you can't. You have to wait for a miracle to happen, and such periods of waiting can be extremely painful.

There are certain things you shouldn't do. Film producers want writers to provide a 'treatment', or a sort of synopsis of events, before they settle down to produce a script. Such treatments are a waste of time, impossible to write and a pain to read. No story can exist until the characters come to life, start to think, feel, talk and play their part in its creation, and don't sit silently sulking in the way Forster described.

I don't think you need to have a whole story in your head before you start writing. You should know, I believe, what you want to say about the human condition. You should have a theme. You should know the place and the characters and probably have an idea of the final destination. And then start to write, because writing pulls down writing in a way that plans and treatments and synopses can never manage. So you can begin anywhere, probably by writing a speech for one or more of the characters, bringing them to life and setting them to work on the plot. If you get them right, they may start to tell a story for you. With any luck you may have the surprising pleasure of writing something which seemed unimportant at the time but turns out to be the very point, the axle on which the story turns. If you get a character right, he or she may tell you what their problem is of their own accord.

If you are very lucky, you may reach that miraculous moment when a character does something that is totally unexpected. You will look at your piece of paper in amazement and think, I never dreamt that you, of all people, would do a thing like that. And then you know that you are on to a thoroughly good thing.

Given the right characters in a situation full of possibilities, the story may begin to tell itself. Of course, it will be up to you to write it, in the voice you will have found which is now, I hope, yours and no one else's. If you're looking for advice on how you should feel when writing, you need look no further than to Muriel Spark, who, in her novel *It's a Far Cry from Kensington*, gave her most precious secrets away.

> You are writing a letter to a friend . . . Write privately, not publicly, without fear or timidity . . . So that your true friend will read it over and over and want more enchanting letters from you. Before starting the letter rehearse in your mind what you are going to tell . . . But don't do too much, the story will develop as you go along, especially if you write to a special friend, man or woman, to make them smile or laugh or cry . . . Remember not to think of the reading public, it will put you off.

Writing like this may give you great pleasure. Even Trigorin in *The Seagull* found it 'pleasant'. But then he had to admit that the worse moment comes when the public reads it: 'Yes, charming and clever, but a long way off Tolstoy.' Or: 'It's a fine thing but Turgenev's *Fathers and Children* did it better.' 'And so,' he says, 'until I drop into my grave it will always be "charming and clever", "charming and clever", nothing more — and after I am dead, acquaintances passing my tomb will say . . . "A fine writer, but he didn't write as well as Turgenev".'

32

The Attestation Clause

Yeats, having made his will on the top of his tower, resolved to compel his soul to study 'in a learned school', until

> *Testy delirium*
> *Or dull decrepitude,*
> *Or what worse evil come —*
> *The death of friends, or death*
> *Of every brilliant eye*
> *That made a catch in the breath —*
> *Seem but the clouds of the sky*
> *When the horizon fades:*
> *Or a bird's sleepy cry*
> *Among the deepening shades.*

It may not be necessary to go through the stage of testy delirium, or even dull decrepitude. Death comes as unexpectedly to the young as it does to the old and our continued existence, Montaigne pointed out, is something of a favour. Both Jesus

Christ and Alexander the Great died at the age of thirty-three. Montaigne then went on to list the many surprising or comical ways in which death can suddenly overtake you. One of the ancestors of the Duke of Brittany, it seems, was killed 'by a bump from a pig'. Another choked to death on a pip from a grape. An emperor died from a scratch when combing his hair. Aeschylus was warned against a falling house and he was always on the alert, but in vain: he was killed by the shell of a tortoise which slipped from the talons of an eagle in flight.

The Lord of Montaigne then lists those who died 'between a woman's thighs'. Among them were a captain of the Roman Guard, the son of Guy di Gonzaga, the Duke of Mantua, a Platonic philosopher and Pope Clement V. Such a death, although no doubt delightful for the man concerned, must have been deeply embarrassing for the woman whose thighs were on offer.

We were in the South of France one year when there was a serious outbreak of forest fires. Small aeroplanes were used to scoop up water from the sea, fly over the burning trees and douse the flames. An innocent and harmless man was happily snorkelling, observing the clouds of bright little fish, when he was scooped up by an aeroplane, carried off and dropped on to a blazing inferno. After writing her death scene, Hardy said that the 'President of the Immortals had ended his sport with Tess'. At least the sport in that case was of a serious, even tragic nature. In the other cases outlined above, the President of the Immortals would seem to be an unprincipled practical joker with a warped sense of humour.

Conscious as he was of falling tortoise-shells and fatal hair combs, and would be now of scooping aeroplanes, Montaigne said he was always prepared for the sudden arrival of death, which might visit him at any hour: 'Being a man who broods over his thoughts and stores them up inside him, I am always just about as ready as I can be when death does suddenly appear.' And he had this advice to give: 'If you have profited from life, and you have had your fill, go away satisfied.' And he ended his message on the subject: 'We must rip the masks off things as well as off people. Once we have done that we shall find underneath only the same death which a valet and a chambermaid got through without being afraid. Blessed the death which gives no time for preparing gatherings of mourners.

★ ★ ★

I seem to have completed my will. I can sign it off and there will be the usual attestation clause, in which the witnesses certify that they have seen me sign in their presence and in the presence of each other.

I have relied on many witnesses, far more than the usual two, to endorse my will. I have placed particular reliance on Shakespeare, Byron, Montaigne, Oscar Wilde, Yeats, Da Ponte and a number of barristers, judges, assorted criminals and companionable women. None of the advice I've offered needs to be taken, none of the likes and dislikes I've displayed have to be shared. There is only one paragraph I'd underline, one truth I hold to be self-evident.

The meaningful and rewarding moments aren't waiting for us beyond the grave, or to be found on distant battlefields where history's made. They can happen quite unexpectedly, in a garden perhaps, or walking through a beech wood in the middle of the afternoon. If we are to have a religion, it should be one that recognizes the true importance of a single moment in time, the instant when you are fully and completely alive.

The rain had fallen steadily out of a grey, gunmetal sky. On 4 January, the day of

Emily's wedding, the sun appeared and shone brightly over the cold countryside. We rode to the village church in a karma car, a somewhat ornate vehicle lined with mirrors, smelling of flowers and incense, a small fleet of which had arrived from Notting Hill Gate. Turville Church has long been part of our lives. My mother and father are buried in the churchyard, which fades into the surrounding fields, as is Lucy, a close childhood friend of Emily's who was tragically killed by a car when she was no more than nine years old. The church was filled to bursting and I managed to walk my daughter reasonably quickly up the aisle as Jon Lord played the music he had written for her on the organ. At the end of the service, Sam Brown, daughter of Joe Brown of The Bruvvers, and her friends sang 'I'm putting all my eggs in one basket'. Emily emerged, married, into the sunlight and, in a shower of confetti, arranged her bouquet on Lucy's grave.

Then we had a party. A tent enveloped the terrace of the house. There was dinner and dancing to a Mexican punk band, friends of Alessandro's who had travelled from Los Angeles to the Chilterns. A small boy, commercially minded, collected autographs from Emily's film-star friends and sold them round the room, insisting on 'hard cash'.

After the fireworks I sat looking at the circular brick platform at the end of the terrace where the Mexican punks were playing and singing. It was where, as an only child, I had done my one-boy shows, having to be both Fred and Ginger or, in my savagely cut version of *Hamlet*, duelling with myself, quarrelling with myself as my own mother, or drinking my own poisoned chalice. It was where Emily had acted plays with her friends from school and here, sometime in the future, another person whose sex was, as yet, unascertained, might be showing off, performing or inventing a story on the same small, circular, open-air stage.

So, at that moment, and what a moment, I could look round at my children and grandchildren, whose ages range from fifty-three to twelve. I could still trace my father's voice in their jokes, their laughter and their way with language. Their words will echo out into the future, with their children and their children's children. It's my father's claim to immortality — and mine also.

It was a day worth passing on in any last will and testament.

About the Author

John Mortimer is the author of twelve collections of Rumpole stories, three acclaimed volumes of autobiography, and numerous novels, including *Rumpole and the Penge Bungalow Murders*. Mortimer, who was knighted in 1998, lives in Oxfordshire, England.